CRE▲TIVE
HOMEOWNER®

POOLS
AND SPAS

PLANNING ▪ DESIGNING ▪ MAINTAINING ▪ LANDSCAPING

FRAN J. DONEGAN
DAVID SHORT

CREATIVE HOMEOWNER®, Upper Saddle River, New Jersey

POOLS & SPAS

AUTHORS	Fran J.Donegan, David Short
SENIOR EDITOR	Kathie Robitz
EDITOR	Therese Hoehlein Cerbie
JUNIOR EDITOR	Jennifer Calvert
EDITORIAL ASSISTANT	Nora Grace
PHOTO RESEARCH	Robyn Poplasky, Jennifer Ramcke, Sharon Ranftle
TECHNICAL REVIEWER	Brian Short
INDEXER	Schroeder Indexing Services
DESIGN AND LAYOUT	David Geer
ILLUSTRATIONS	Vincent Babak (all, unless otherwise noted); Nancy Hull (pp. 18, 24,159, 162, 171); Glee Barre(pp. 26–27); Rick Daskam (p. 165); Robert LaPointe (p. 175)
FRONT COVER PHOTOGRAPHY	(top) Ken Druse; (bottom right & left center) Steven Wooster/Garden Picture Library; (bottom left) Brett Drury
BACK COVER PHOTOGRAPHY	(bottom right) Palma Allen; (top left both) John Parsekian/CH; (center left) Mark Lohman

CREATIVE HOMEOWNER

VICE PRESIDENT AND PUBLISHER	Timothy O. Bakke
PRODUCTION DIRECTOR	Kimberly H. Vivas
ART DIRECTOR	David Geer
MANAGING EDITOR	Fran J. Donegan

Current Printing (last digit)
10 9 8 7 6 5 4 3 2 1

Pools & Spas: Planning, Designing, Maintaining, and Landscaping, Second Edition
Library of Congress Control Number: 2007933857
ISBN-10: 1-58011-391-5
ISBN-13: 978-1-58011-391-5

CREATIVE HOMEOWNER®
A Division of Federal Marketing Corp.
24 Park Way
Upper Saddle River, NJ 07458
www.creativehomeowner.com

dedication

We would like to thank the Association of Pool and Spa Professionals for its generosity in supplying information used in this book. We would also like to thank the editorial staff of Creative Homeowner for the hours of hard work that went into producing *Pools & Spas*. Special thanks go to senior editor Kathie Robitz, Terry Cerbie, designer David Geer, assistant editors Jennifer Ramcke and Sharon Ranftle, and junior editor Jennifer Calvert.

In memory of David Short
1956–2005

contents

introduction

I t wasn't so long ago that owning an in-ground pool, a large aboveground swimming pool, or a spa was considered the height of luxury. Pools were synonymous with big houses and even bigger family fortunes. That is not true anymore. Today, backyard swimming pools and spas are increasingly becoming popular. New materials, innovative building techniques, the variety of products, and intense competition among manufacturers and builders have put pools and spas within the reach of many people. It is not unusual for the backyard of the most ordinary house on the block to contain a large in-ground or aboveground pool surrounded by a landscaped deck with a bubbling spa or hot tub.

But while pools and spas are becoming more common, they are not so commonplace that they don't require some thought and work from you, the homeowner. Building a pool or spa or, more likely, having one built is one of those projects that takes place maybe once or twice in a lifetime for most homeowners. Yet the process requires knowledge of a variety of subjects, an awareness of what is available, decision-making ability, and patience. You will need to do all that while dealing with a large industry made up of many small and varied parts. The scope of what is involved often makes finding reliable information difficult—but not impossible with *Pools & Spas*.

This book is designed for homeowners who have decided to take the plunge into owning a pool or spa and need an education on the subject. It is also for those who aren't quite sure whether or not a pool or spa is for them but want to gather more information before making a final decision. The book is organized in much the same way as the process of having a pool or spa installed. It begins with the planning stages and proceeds through construction, maintenance, landscaping ideas, and pool and spa safety. There's even a chapter devoted to saunas.

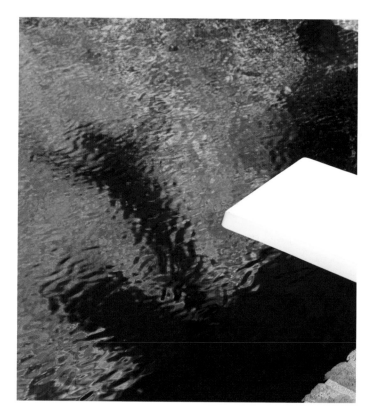

Diving into one's own backyard pool, above, has become an increasingly affordable luxury for many homeowners.

A deck or patio for sunning, relaxing, and entertaining will probably be a key element in your new pool design plan, below.

THE PLANNING STAGES

Chapter 1, "Getting Your Feet Wet—Planning Your Pool & Spa," introduces you to the subject, including tips on selecting the best type of pool or spa for you and your family. You will be surprised at how many different kinds are available. Information found here will help you assess your yard with regard to slope, shape, and soil composition. It will also get you started in sketching out plans for your private recreation area. In addition, the chapter contains a primer on hiring and working with pool companies.

Selecting a pool or spa means dealing with all of the options open to you, and *Pools & Spas* puts you right in among all of those choices. Chapter 2, "Diving In—Pool & Spa Styles," outlines the pros and cons of the materials used in building or manufacturing pools and spas. There are more materials available to you than you may be aware of, and they all have different building requirements. Armed with the information in this chapter you will be able to select the products that best suit your needs.

Some parts of the pool and spa buying and building experience are more enjoyable than others. Many people find the planning and selection processes more fun than choosing the equipment—the pumps, filters, and heaters—that is the subject of Chapter 3, "Pool Gear—Pool & Spa Equipment." The good news is that if you are working with a qualified builder or dealer, he or she can size and select the equipment. The better news is that this chapter will give you the background to make sure you get the best components.

Not all pool and spa equipment is of equal importance. Some, such as the pump-and-filtration system, are necessary. Your local building codes may require they be part of your project. Other types of equipment, however, are not necessary but they can increase your enjoyment. In Chapter 4, "Enhancing the Experience—Accessories and Fun Stuff," you will find information on timers, lights, slides, shade accessories, and much more.

A palm-thatched cabana reminiscent of a tropical beach resort, below, provides a shady retreat next to this contemporary pool.

THE REALITY OF BUILDING AND MAINTENANCE

With ownership comes responsibility. Chapter 5, "Sparkling Water—Pool Chemistry Made Easy," prepares you for what you'll need to know about water treatment, including some alternatives to traditional Chlorine. You will learn how to adjust the components in your pool and spa water to make and keep them clean. You won't learn enough to become a chemist, but after reading these chapters you will know how to react to the conditions in your pool or spa to make swimming or soaking a pleasant and healthy experience.

Although you may be capable of building a pool or installing a spa, this isn't a construction guide. Rather, it is a buyer's guide that provides the information you need to make intelligent purchasing decisions. Chapter 6, "Creating Your Dream—The ABCs of Building Pools & Spas," does not offer step-by-step building procedures but is designed to let you know what to expect during the process.

But there may be some projects you will want to tackle on your own. For example, you may wish to install your own aboveground pool or put in a portable spa—both projects that a competent do-it-yourselfer can handle. Fortunately, the manufacturers of these types of projects provide installation instructions, and we provide some installation tips to help make the project go smoother.

Chapter 7, "Pool Keeping—Routine Maintenance & Care," outlines a simple schedule for you or your pool service to follow. You'll learn what needs to be done to open the pool for the season, keep it clean throughout the year, and then close it down for the cold weather, if necessary.

You'll get more enjoyment from your new pool if it is easily accessible from the house, left; make sure you can readily reach it through a family room, living room, or kitchen.

Many of today's new pool and spa designs capture the free-form beauty of natural rock formations and waterfalls, above.

COMPLETING YOUR PROJECT

This contemporary pool and spa, above, is perfectly situated to take advantage of the spectacular view.

Soft cushions surrounding this spa, below, are a welcome touch that encourages conversation and relaxation.

Chapter 8, "Around the Pool—Landscaping and Water Features," provides ideas for poolside decks and patios, tips on selecting plants that work well with pool areas, and ways to create a private, attractive, and relaxing environment. You will need the information in this chapter to plan the overall project, but it is also a good reference to review once the building crews have left. In it you will find design ideas for decks, patios, walkways, ponds, waterfalls, and fountains.

Chapter 9, "Worry-Free Fun—Using Your Pool & Spa Safely," may be the most important chapter in the book. It deals with pool safety and provides practical, real-life suggestions for keeping those who swim in your pool or soak in your spa safe. It is a good idea to review this chapter at the start of every swimming season.

Finally, Chapter 10, "Soothing Saunas—A Healthy Habit," covers the information that you will need to purchase a sauna. As you will see, a sauna can complement a new swimming pool whether it's used for relaxing or as part of a health regimen.

CHAPTER 1

Getting Your Feet Wet

Pools and spas are fun, but there can be hassles building and installing them. So let's begin with an important piece of advice: before you play, do a little homework. Start by thinking of your new pool or spa for what it really is—a major home improvement project that is going to require you to make decisions, hire professionals, maybe do some of the work yourself and, of course, pay the bills.

No matter which type of pool or spa you choose, it will be only one element in the overall design of your outdoor living space. You may want to build a deck or patio around the pool for sunning and entertaining, install lighting, add new landscaping, and perhaps add a shed or an outbuilding for storing equipment or changing in and out of swimwear. Hot tubs and spas require the same considerations, but usually on a smaller scale.

However, your home paradise doesn't have to be done all at once. Some things, such as a large multilevel redwood deck or a flagstone patio enclosed by a garden wall, can be postponed. Just be sure to allot the necessary space for them. But it is a good idea to rough-in pool-related items, such as heaters or fountains, that you may want to add in the future. It is generally more expensive if you do a major renovation later. Chapter 8, "Around the Pool—Landscaping and Water Features," beginning on page 156, contains more useful information on that topic.

USES FOR YOUR POOL AND SPA

How you plan to use your pool and spa will help determine the type of pool and spa you will need. Throw the dimensions of your yard into the equation, and you should be able to come up with a rough plan that gives an idea of the size and shape of pool and spa that is right for you, as well as some idea about where to put them in your yard. Of course, there is a lot more to think about, including your budget, but start slowly. Before you begin working on the details, think of the big picture. Start the planning process by thinking about the things you and your family enjoy the most. Here are some ideas.

A Recreation Center

This is probably the most popular type of pool. It's where you and your family and friends hang out and have some good wet fun. If spending an afternoon splashing around on a float is your idea of a swim, perhaps an aboveground pool might be for you. Or you can opt for an in-ground pool that has a constant depth—let's say about 4 feet. Both are good choices, especially if small children will be using the pool. The depth accommodates most pool games and is still enough to swim for exercise.

A large pool with a deep end for diving becomes shallower toward the far end. Note the vanishing edge.

If you decide to add a diving board, the pool will need a deep end. Recommendations vary, but plan on a depth of about 9 to 11 feet in the diving area, which should extend out a minimum of approximately 12 feet in front of the diving board.

Other amenities to consider for a recreation center include slides and a nearby spa.

Lap Pools

Lap pools are for those who want to exercise regularly by swimming. A 3½-foot shallow end and 5-foot deep end is typical. An Olympic-size pool is 25 meters long—a little over 82 feet. Most yards don't have that kind of space, but if you can accommodate a pool that is 30 to 40 feet long or more and 8 to 10 feet wide, you will be able to do some serious training. The pool should have flat, parallel walls and a painted or tiled lap line and turning targets in the floor.

For those who don't want to swim laps but plan on doing water aerobics, length isn't important. As long as the pool is 4 feet deep, you'll get a good workout.

Of course, nothing says you can't have a pool that lets you do both: float away a hot afternoon, and train for the next Olympics. If you have the space in your yard, it is possible to combine the long, narrow shape of the typical lap pool with a large constant-depth area for pool games.

A Swim Spa. Another choice for exercise buffs is a swim spa. This is a small pool—some models are only 10 to 14 feet long—that produces a strong artificial current against which you can swim without moving forward. This action is sometimes called "treadmill swimming." Both lap pools and swim spas are great choices for indoor exercise areas.

Besides providing an exercise area, a swim spa is a compact alternative to a full-size in-ground pool. It will work well in a narrow yard, and unlike a full-size lap pool, it doesn't require an open stretch of ground.

Lap pools, above right, are 8 to 10 feet wide and are usually 4 feet deep.

A swim spa, right, provides a current against which to swim for people who want a healthy workout.

A Relaxation Center

A good soak in a swimming pool can certainly relax you. But to relieve the tensions of the day or pamper sore muscles, nothing beats a session in a spa or hot tub. Many people who build a pool include either an in-ground or portable spa as part of the package. As with pools, there is a lot to choose from here. In-ground versions complement the design of the larger pool. Usually, they are built right next to the pool where they share pumps, filters, and heaters. Portable spas give you the option of placing the spa in some other part of the yard, such as on an existing deck or patio, where it is easier to reach from the house. Portable spas are self-contained units with pumps, filters, a heater, and sometimes lighting built right into the unit.

A portable spa, above, comes with numerous jets to massage and relax muscles.

A hot tub, below, offers a deeper soak—as much as 4 ft.—than other types of spas.

Smart Tip

Give the idea of a pool with a deep end serious thought. In my experience, most homeowners don't need deep pools. These models are more expensive to build and maintain, and there are obvious safety factors to consider. Also, it is tough to have a decent pool volleyball game when one team is in 4 feet of water while the other team is in 6 feet.—D.S.

CREATE A PLAN

If you've thought about installing a pool or spa, you probably have a general idea about where to place it in your yard. A pool or spa is going to be the focus of an outdoor living area, so it should be in a convenient spot. Like a deck or patio, it should have a connection to the house. You will gravitate to the area more readily if you can reach the new pool through a public room such as family room or kitchen. Also, it is usually easier to keep an eye on what is going on in the pool from these frequented parts of the

A pool attracts a crowd, so it's wise to locate it where access to the house is easy.

house. Little-used areas, such as a bedroom in the middle of the day, do not make good entry points for the pool area, but might be ideal for gaining access to a private, enclosed spa or hot tub.

Smart Tip

A complaint I hear from homeowners is that they wish they had put the pool closer to the house. A pool that is close makes entertaining and bringing food and drinks from the house—and cleaning up after a party—much easier.—D.S.

Having a general idea of where to locate your pool or spa is a good start, but there are a number of other considerations to keep in mind. The best way to approach this stage of the planning is to draw a plot plan of your property on graph paper. This will give you a scaled-down overhead view that should show the location of all of the existing elements, such as the house, driveway, lawns, gardens, trees, decks, and any other outdoor structures. If you'll be adding other features, the plan will also help you to allot the proper space and location for them on your site.

If you plan to do landscaping simultaneously with pool construction, you might want to include these plans as well, perhaps on a separate copy or on a tissue-paper overlay with the pool and spa in place. At the very least, you will have begun the process of determining your future plans for the area surrounding the pool or spa. (See Chapter 8, "Around the Pool—Landscaping and Water Features", page 156, for more information.)

Survey Maps

An alternative is to create a base map from a copy of your plot (or property survey) prepared by surveyors, which most homeowners receive when they purchase their house. You can also request one from your tax assessor's office. Copies are usually available at no cost or for a nominal fee. A surveyor's map will save you time taking measurements. In addition to showing property lines, a footprint on the house, and other significant structures, the plan should show easements and the location of overhead and underground utility lines. Make enlarged copies of the plat so that you can draw on them, or use one copy as a base and add tissue layers to draw in the other components.

A dramatic rounded edge helps this pool fit into the overall design scheme of this yard.

CREATE A BASE MAP

Working with an enlarged copy of a surveyor's map of your property is a smart idea because it already contains accurate measurements, boundary lines, and your house.

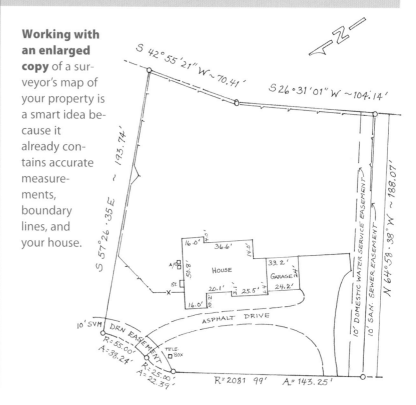

This natura-listic design, left, integrates stone, trees, and a man-made water-fall into the pool scape.

At a proper distance, a cluster of trees, below, provides privacy without blocking sunlight from the water.

Items to Include in a Plan

Several features will work together to give you a clear picture of your site and help you to determine the best location for your pool or spa. It's important to include all of them in your plan.

Existing Structures. In addition to the house and garage, indicate tool sheds, decks, patios, and any existing fences. Make note of all paved surfaces, such as driveways and walkways.

Trees and Shrubs. Draw in all of the shrubs and trees on your property. It is important to keep the location of trees and shrubs in mind when placing your pool. They can provide shade or act as a windbreak if it's needed. Avoid placing pools and spas under trees so that you are not continually scooping out leaves from the water. Even the needles from conifers can become a maintenance problem. Existing trees and shrubs can be relocated or removed, but that will increase the cost of your project.

Buried Utilities. Mark underground gas, sewer, water, and electric lines after consulting with your utility companies and local building department for the exact locations. Don't forget to indicate septic tanks and leech fields on your plan as well. Also, make note of any overhead power lines that cross your property. It is illegal to build a pool under power lines.

Soil Conditions. Soil type is a factor to consider before selecting a site for a pool. Soil that is too sandy will be difficult to excavate because it won't hold a shape; too much clay tends to expand when it gets wet. Don't worry if you can't tell whether the soil is sandy or contains a lot of clay; the pool builder can make that judgment. But it will help if he can get information from you that's only available through long-term observation, such as if there are areas in the yard where water tends to pond after a rain shower.

Pool builders can compensate for these soil conditions. They can sink piers down to firm bedrock to support a pool in unstable soil. Faced with clay, they can surround the pool with soft fill material to absorb any expansion.

Siting a pool takes into account several factors, including soil quality and the slope of the land.

Slope of the Land. The slope of the landscape must also be taken into consideration. In general, surface water should drain away from the pool. You should avoid situations where surface runoff flows into the pool. If you have a flat yard or even one where small amounts of water puddle, you can bring in topsoil to create a gentle slope away from the pool.

The contractor may also suggest a drainage system for the area around the pool. A subsurface drainage system may also be necessary if naturally occurring ground water keeps the soil wet. The system, which is usually perforated drainage pipe buried in gravel, may be able to divert water away from the pool area.

Sun and Wind Patterns. You will get a lot more enjoyment from your pool if you pay attention to how the sun and wind affect your site. Keep in mind that in the northern hemisphere, the sun's arc during the day follows a southerly course. In summer, the sun seems to be high

SUN AND SHADE

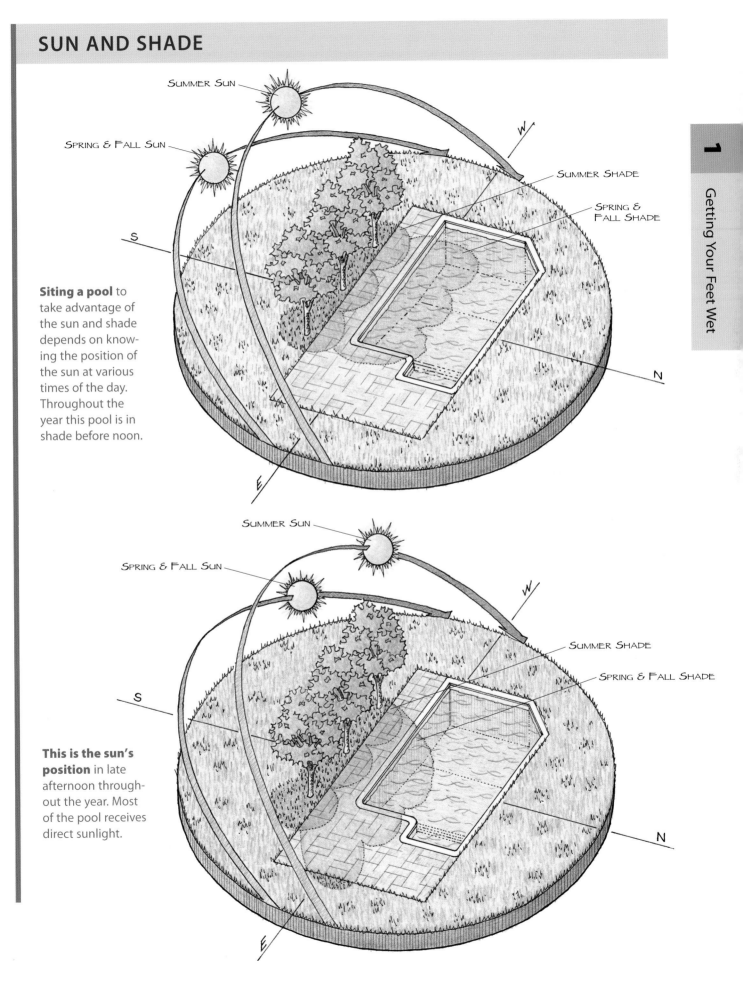

SUMMER SUN

SPRING & FALL SUN

W

SUMMER SHADE

SPRING & FALL SHADE

S

N

E

Siting a pool to take advantage of the sun and shade depends on knowing the position of the sun at various times of the day. Throughout the year this pool is in shade before noon.

SUMMER SUN

SPRING & FALL SUN

W

SUMMER SHADE

SPRING & FALL SHADE

S

N

This is the sun's position in late afternoon throughout the year. Most of the pool receives direct sunlight.

E

overhead. In winter, the sun tracks lower in the sky. The sun is usually at its hottest in the late afternoon when it is sinking in the west. If your pool or spa is open to these directions, it will receive the maximum warmth from the sun.

Whether or not that is a good thing depends on where you live. In hot climates, the afternoon sun can be unbearable. By the same logic, a pool or spa always in the shade in the north could be just as unpleasant much of the time. The goal is to consider the prevailing local conditions when choosing a site for your pool. If the spot you had in mind doesn't get much sun and you live in Minnesota, you may want to find another location—perhaps one where most of the pool would be exposed to the sun in the late afternoon. Or, if possible, you may want to consider removing whatever is causing the shade.

A strong wind or even a stiff breeze blowing across the surface of the pool can make swimming uncomfortable. The same is true for the location of a spa. Fortunately, you can divert the wind with clumps of plantings, fences, or even the placement of a small enclosed structure, such as an equipment shed or changing cabana.

A wall of hedges and other dense plantings offers privacy and serves as a windbreak.

WIND PROTECTION

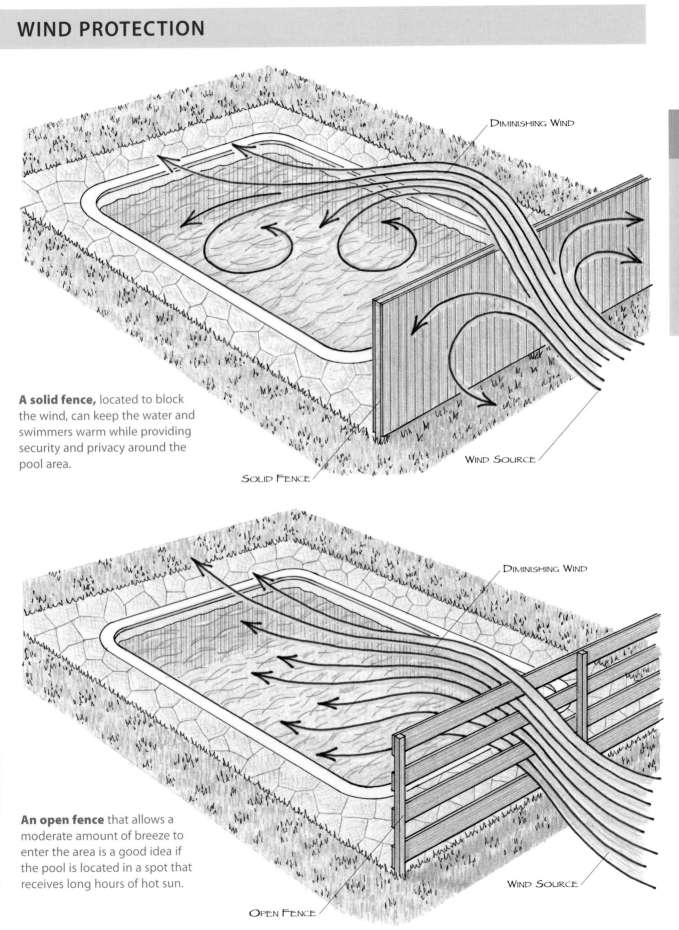

DIMINISHING WIND

A solid fence, located to block the wind, can keep the water and swimmers warm while providing security and privacy around the pool area.

SOLID FENCE

WIND SOURCE

DIMINISHING WIND

An open fence that allows a moderate amount of breeze to enter the area is a good idea if the pool is located in a spot that receives long hours of hot sun.

OPEN FENCE

WIND SOURCE

ADDING THE POOL OR SPA TO YOUR PLAN

Once you have a plan of your yard and all of its important elements, you can begin experimenting with locations for the pool. Don't be too worried about getting everything perfect at this stage. Your pool builder will have suggestions about where to locate the pool, too. But this exercise will help you get started on the overall design of your yard with the pool or spa in it.

Try to be as accurate as possible when drawing the plan. That means you will probably need to take some measurements. Rather than drawing straight lines, you can use a series of ovals and circles to show the relative size of components and their relationship to other things in the yard. No one would be able to actually build from such a plan, but these sketches can be a starting point. Once you have the plan on paper you can pencil in the location of the pool or spa.

There are also home-design software products on the market that you can use. The software is fairly inexpensive and lets you place standard objects such as trees and decks with a touch of a button. You can also move things around

WORKING THE POOL INTO THE BASE MAP

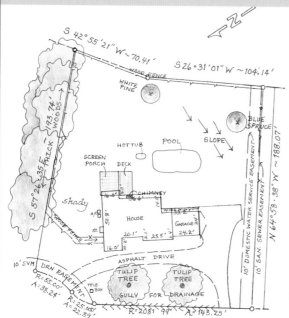

◀ **Experiment** with the location of the pool and spa by simply indicating them on a copy of the base map. Use a circle or an oval that approximates their size and position in relationship to the house and the rest of the landscape.

▶ **Embellish the plan** with any additional features or elements you want to include as part of an overall design for your outdoor area, such as a patio, deck, or screened porch. Although this isn't a formal working plan, it is a good idea to take accurate measurements so that you can get a good picture on paper.

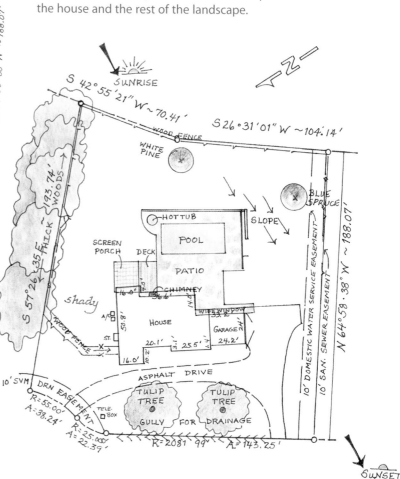

easier on the computer than if you are working by hand.

Computer software lets you easily create and alter a number of plans quickly once you become familiar with the software. However, if you prefer the traditional method of paper and pencil, use tracing paper to sketch out the pool or spa, and anything else, such as a deck or patio, that will be added around it.

Practical Realities

While it is okay to daydream about long, lazy afternoons in your new pool or spa, you can't ignore the practical realities of everyday life. Adding a pool or spa to your yard will change the way you use your outdoor living area. Plan for these changes now, before work actually begins. Here are some things to think about.

Privacy. This is often a concern of pool and spa owners. On most suburban building lots the backyard isn't visible from the street. But if that isn't the case, pay particular attention to where you need to shield the view and how you can add privacy. Items to consider include plantings of tall shrubs and trees or fencing.

And don't forget your neighbor's privacy and comfort. Placing a pool, spa, or its equipment too close to the property line may not be in the best interests of friendship and peaceful coexistence.

WORKING WITH UNUSUAL-SHAPED LOTS

On a long narrow lot, a freeform pool at one end of the lot and substantial plantings create a balance of indoor and outdoor living spaces. Pavers visually unite the house, spa, and pool.

On a shallow lot, a rectangular pool fits nicely into the landscape behind the house. Paving around the pool extends to the adjacent patio to expand the recreation area.

An angular-shaped lot benefits from a kidney shaped pool with an attached in-ground spa and patio. The large, curvaceous pool makes the most of the wide end of this backyard.

POOL SHAPES

Basic Pool Shapes

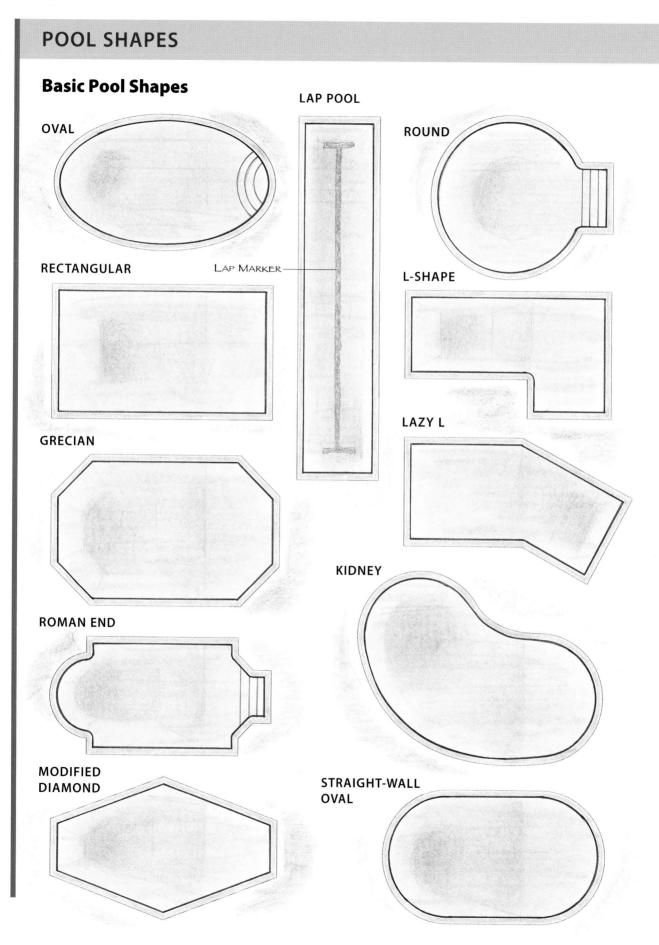

OVAL

LAP POOL

ROUND

RECTANGULAR

LAP MARKER

L-SHAPE

GRECIAN

LAZY L

ROMAN END

KIDNEY

MODIFIED DIAMOND

STRAIGHT-WALL OVAL

Freeform Pool Shapes

SPA

SPA

SPA

SPA

LAP MARKER

Access to Electric and Water Services. You will need both of these for the finished pool or spa and while the work is underway. You may have to upgrade electrical service to accommodate the various pumps, filters, and other accessories that are part of a new pool or spa. At the very least, plan on an electrician running dedicated circuits to the pool area. In some cases, he can run the circuit from the existing electric panel. But if the panel is full or nearly full, which means all of the possible circuit locations are already

A lap pool meets a wider pool area that is more suitable to game playing and water sports.

occupied, you may need a boost in service. That means that an electrician, working with your utility company, will add circuits to bring more power into your home. Also, be aware that electric lines must not cross over the pool. Discuss your options with your pool dealer and an electrician.

You will need water to fill your pool, but you will also

need water to maintain it. A garden hose that reaches your pool is adequate in most cases. For large in-ground pools, builders can add an automatic fill line that attaches to your existing water supply pipes.

Water is also necessary to clean and maintain pumps and filters. Many people overlook this requirement and end up snaking garden hoses across the yard to clean a filter. If your equipment will be located away from the house, have a water line installed during pool construction to make maintenance easier.

Access for Building Equipment. In-ground pools, in particular, require the use of heavy equipment. Backhoes, trucks, and other heavy equipment all require access into your yard. That means a clearance that's about 10 feet wide. You should also plan access for the removal or secondary use of any dirt, rocks, or debris that is the result of the construction.

An in-ground pool and spa, requires the use of heavy equipment during construction.

BUILDING PERMITS AND BUILDING CODES

YOUR TOWN may require you to apply for a building permit before starting construction on your pool. If you are doing the work yourself, call the building department to find out whether a permit is necessary. If a pool or spa company is handling the job, make sure that the contract states that the builder is responsible for securing all of the necessary permits.

Although procedures may vary from town to town, applying for a permit sets in motion a number of events. First, the building department will review your plans. Later, the building inspector may also want to visit the site to make sure that the project complies with zoning laws.

Building codes are complex documents that state minimum construction requirements for people's safety. They can vary from town to town. Some communities have code requirements for pools and spas, and many address some of the things that may go along with a new one, such as safety fences, decks, patios, and electrical work.

A reputable pool company should be familiar with the requirements in your area. But as the homeowner you are responsible for the project. At the very least, discuss the need for permits and code requirements with the contractor before signing the contract. If you are not satisfied, look for another contractor.

REVIEW LOCAL ZONING LAWS

MUNICIPALITIES CREATE ZONING LAWS to control how land is used in a given area. In the broadest sense, they separate residential from industrial and commercial areas. This distinction also means that Company X can't build an asphalt plant on your block. But local zoning laws can also affect how you use your own property. Some things to check on while still in the planning stage for your pool or spa include *height restrictions for fences* and *required setbacks* (or the distance between your property line and the structures you want to build).

If your plans don't comply with local regulations, either make the necessary changes or apply for a zoning variance. Zoning laws are written in very general terms that are open to interpretation for specific projects. The zoning board or commissioner will decide whether to issue the variance or reject the appeal. Ask about your local variance procedure at the building or planning department. Basically, you will need to prove to a zoning board that your plans will not harm your neighbors or encroach on their privacy. The variance process can take time, so it's best to learn the zoning regulations early.

Time spent relaxing in a spa is especially enjoyable after an aerobic swim in a pool.

NOW OR ADD LATER?

BUILDING A POOL OR SPA is a lot like building or renovating a house. You can build or add everything at once, or you can take care of the main area now and add on later.

Here are the items you should include during construction or installation. Some are absolutely necessary, while others are optional or just easier to install at this stage.

- Pumps
- Filters
- Ladders/handrails
- Steps
- Diving boards (optional)
- Slides (optional)
- Fill lines (optional)
- Covers
- Safety items
- Lights (optional)
- Sound system (optional)
- Maintenance equipment and/or maintenance contract

Here are some elements you can add to your pool or spa later:

- Heaters
- Automatic cleaners
- Decks and patios
- Landscaping
- Automatic controls
- Time clocks
- Shade structures
- Chemical feeders

An indoor pool, like the lap pool and spa above, lets you take control of the environment year-round.

Modern architecture, below, with its connectedness to the outdoors, easily incorporates a pool into its design.

FINANCING THE PROJECT

You may have seen advertisements that tout, "Above-ground pools starting at $499," or, "Own this in-ground pool for $7,000, this four-person spa for $2999.99." If you rely on that hype to set your budget, you are in for a shock when the final bill arrives. Having a new pool or spa installed rarely means making one purchase. Even if the above-ground pool mentioned in the ad includes a pump and filter as part of the package, there is still decking and ladders to consider. A portable spa with jets, a pump, filter, and controls built into the cabinet has to go somewhere. If it's on a deck, the deck may require reinforcement or a concrete pad installed for a level, stable installation.

Other Cost Considerations

The cost of your pool or spa does not stop with its purchase and installation. Besides maintenance costs and yearly service contracts, there are two additional expenses to plan for: insurance premiums and property taxes.

Find out what the addition of a pool or spa will add to the cost of your homeowner's insurance. Be sure your agent is aware of any safety features you will be including in the project, such as fences with locked gates, pool safety covers, and alarms, which may reduce rates.

A new pool will increase the value of your property. That's the good news; the bad news in many parts of the country is that an increase in property value also means an increase in property taxes.

Remember also to plan for your later expenses—the cost of that magnificent deck or patio, the outdoor furniture, the light and sound systems—that you will want or need to fully enjoy your pool or spa.

Before you dive in, remember that adding a pool to your property may raise your property taxes.

Getting the Money

Depending on your circumstances, you will have to weigh the pros and cons of any financing arrangement. As a first step, discuss your plans with a financial advisor.

Personal Savings. Taking money from savings means that you won't pay finance charges, which can be considerable. But it also means that you must have the money to begin with and that once it's out of your hands, it's gone.

Home Equity. You can tap into your property's equity in two ways: refinance your present mortgage, or take on a second mortgage. Before doing either, compare the terms and conditions of several financial institutions.

If your property has appreciated in value, you may be able to refinance your current mortgage for an amount that will pay off your old mortgage, include the cost of the pool, and still allow you to maintain at least 20-percent equity in the market value of your home. Mortgage rates are generally lower than other loan rates, and the interest you pay is tax deductible. In a competitive loan market, mortgage lenders often allow you to refinance up to 100 percent of the value of the property. But if you don't retain at least 20 percent equity in the property, you will be forced to pay a Private Mortgage Insurance (PMI) premium each month with the mortgage payment. PMI is not tax deductible nor does it reduce the principle of the loan.

A second mortgage and a home equity line of credit are two other ways to finance a pool project. Although both are technically second mortgages, there are differences. With the former, you receive a lump sum and make regular payments. With the latter, you write checks on an amount of money made available to you. You pay interest on the amount you spend. Many lines of credit require only the payment of interest during the life of the line with a lump-sum payment due at the end, which is usually 10 or 20 years. Or the amount you borrowed is converted to a standard loan. Of course, the sooner you pay off the loan, the less interest you will pay. Like a first mortgage, interest paid on a second mortgage may be tax deductible. And like a first mortgage, your home is security for the loan. Failure to make payments could mean the loss of your property.

Other Methods. Personal loans are available through banks. They generally carry a higher interest rate, and the interest is not tax deductible. Larger pool dealers sometimes offer financing.

Some local codes may require you to build a fence, such as the one above, around a yard with a pool.

You can add style with tile, below, but that detail will expand the bottom line, too.

HIRING A CONTRACTOR

Back at the beginning of this chapter you learned that you should think of your new pool as a major remodeling project. Finding a good pool company is much the same as hiring a contractor to add an addition to your home or redo your kitchen. The goal here is to find and get bids from at least three companies that you think would do a good job.

Ask Friends for References

Start by finding out the name of the contractor who built the pools of your friends and relatives. Another alternative is to be bold and ask people you don't know but whose pools or spas you like. Ask them about their experiences in working with the contractor. For an idea of the questions to pose, see "What to Ask Your Friends about Their Contractor," on the next page. While you're at it, ask them whom they use to service and maintain their pool or spa.

Smart Tip

Servicing the pool and spa is more important than people realize, especially if they have never owned a pool before. So when selecting a pool or spa company, consider the level of service the company will offer down the road.—D.S.

Find Your Own

If you can't come up with three contractors through the recommendations of others, you will need to prequalify contractors on your own. One way to do this is simply to look in the local phone book for the names and numbers of pool companies. You can also contact the Association of Pool and Spa Professionals (APSP) a professional organization for pool builders and dealers. (See the Resource Guide at the end of this book.) Being a member of an organization like NSPI shows a certain level of commitment to the industry. It does not mean that members are necessarily the best pool companies around, but it does mean that they are serious about their business.

Check Them Out

Once you have put a list of pool companies together, do a little detective work before you even contact them. Visit their showrooms and offices to see what type of investment they have made in their business. Take note of the parts and accessories they have in stock or make readily available to pool or spa owners.

Check with the Better Business Bureau for complaints about the company. Some local bureaus are better than others about gathering and disseminating information concerning businesses, but it is a good place to start. Don't be put off by one or two complaints against a company. Not all complaints are valid. But if there are a number of them, it's probably best to steer clear.

A solar-heated pool may be affordable and energy efficient. It may also extend the swimming season by a couple of months, especially if you live in a northern climate.

If the company's advertisement states that it is part of a a professional organization, contact the group and verify that membership. If the company lists a Web site, check that out. You probably won't find any negative information there, but you may be able to get a "feel" for the company. For example, you may learn how long the company has been in business and the types of projects in which it specializes. Many of these Web sites also post a gallery of pools the company has installed.

Interview each potential contractor, just like any other employer would. Invite each one to your home to inspect the site and discuss the project. Try to gauge how well he listens to your ideas and communicates his to you. For an idea of what questions to ask, review the list on page 36, "What to Ask Potential Contractors. "

WHAT TO ASK YOUR FRIENDS ABOUT THEIR CONTRACTOR

- **Did he complete the job at the agreed-upon price?**
- **Did he complete the job in a timely fashion?**
- **Did he clean up at the end of the day, or did he leave debris in the work area?**
- **Did you have a good working relationship with the contractor?**
- **Did the contractor assign one person to be your contact?**
- **Would you hire that contractor again?**

1

Getting Your Feet Wet

FINDING A SPA DEALER

THE SPA AND HOT TUB SEGMENT of the pool industry is growing by leaps and bounds. And why not? Much of what you hear is absolutely true: they are fun, relaxing, and a great addition to anyone's outdoor living area. Although there are a few bad products on the market, many of the good products are sold by people who are not qualified to service them properly.

When selecting a spa dealer, make sure the company can also service the unit. You should also feel confident that the dealer knows enough about his product to answer any questions you have about its routine maintenance. It is difficult to keep the water in a spa clean and sanitary, and as a new owner you may require advice from time to time. (For more information, see Chapter 2, "Diving In— Pool and Spa Styles," on page 38.)

Filtering, heating, and disinfecting the water is important spa maintenance.

Collect Estimates

Contractors will submit estimates of what they think your project will cost. Then it's up to you to compare them. Ideally, all of the contractors with whom you speak should have the same information about the project and its parameters when they prepare their estimates. Remember, even if you know exactly what you want, a good contractor will make suggestions to improve the project, and an experienced salesman will try to sell you an upgrade. So it really isn't prudent or fair to compare one contractor's bid against another's unless all of the details are the same. If you like one contractor's suggestions and want to add them to your original plans, inform all of the parties who are preparing bids so that you can obtain the most accurate estimates for the job.

With the estimates in hand, the impressions you have of the companies you've contacted, and the information you've gained from contacting their references, you can make a decision. There are a lot of theories about how to do this. Some people say toss out the lowest bid because the contractor is trying to lowball you into getting the job, and then will raise his price later while he's building. That is possible, but if a bid is much lower than the others, make sure that contractor has all the information he needs to prepare the estimate. He may simply have left something out of his original calculations.

One theory holds that a company that does everything itself without the use of subcontractors is better than one that relies on subs. That is a matter of opinion. Some installations require the skills of a number of different trades. If one company does everything, then the people working there need to have a variety of skills. Are those people better at their jobs than a subcontractor that specializes in one trade and does it everyday? It is a tricky question, especially in areas where skilled labor is in short supply. Ask the contractor or dealer if he uses subcontractors. If he says yes, ask how long he has worked with them. A smart dealer tends to stay with a subcontractor who does a good job on a consistent basis. Then make it clear that you intend to deal directly with the contractor or dealer with whom you are making the deal, not with the subcontractors.

The Contract

There should always be a written contract for any in-ground installation. Some aboveground pools also require one if the dealer is doing the installation. If you are not sure, put any contract exceeding $1,000 in writing.

Read the contract carefully. Under federal law, you have three business days after signing to change your mind.

Stone decking, opposite, creates a natural transition from water to lawn and emphasizes the pool's shape.

WHAT TO ASK POTENTIAL CONTRACTORS

- **Is he properly licensed and insured? Ask to see proof of both. You are looking for Workmen's Compensation and liability insurance.**
- **Can he provide a list of references? Check them out personally.**
- **How long has he been in business in the area?**
- **Is there enough clearance on the property for his equipment?**
- **Will any plantings or structures need to be removed during the construction process?**
- **When can he begin the project?**

- **Who will be your contact within the company?**
- **Will he provide a written estimate? If not, that may be a signal to move on to another company.**
- **Can he provide a blank copy of his standard contract? This will give you a head start on studying the contract. You will be able to see what types of things are included and what might have been left out. In other words, you will be ready to make additions or deletions to the contract should you decide to sign with his company.**

WHAT EVERY CONTRACT SHOULD CONTAIN

CONTRACTS FOR THE INSTALLATION of a pool or spa should always include the following items:

• A description of the work to be performed, including the brand name and model number of all pumps, filters, and the like that will be installed as part of the project.

• The agreed-upon cost of the project and a payment schedule. Don't pay the entire amount up front. In some states, it is illegal for the contractor to request more than $1,000 or 10 percent of the project as a down payment. Withhold the final payment until the work is completed to your satisfaction.

• The start and completion dates. Some contractors will balk at specifying a completion date, but you should request one. If you do, remember you will have to make allowances for the weather.

• An agreement that the contractor will obtain all the necessary permits.

• An agreement that the contractor will pay all subcontractors and suppliers promptly, and that he will provide lien releases from all subcontractors. If a contractor fails to pay a subcontractor, the payee can place a lien on your property. A lien release states that the subcontractor has been paid in full.

CHAPTER 2

Diving In

There are two ways to choose your new pool or spa. The first is to learn as much as you can about the options available and then weigh them against the needs and wishes of you and your family. The second option is to simply pick a pool builder and let him decide. Most pool installers specialize in building one or, at the most, two types of pools. In essence, once you've selected a contractor, you've picked the type of pool that will be installed in your yard.

The first option seems best. Not only will you end up with the pool or spa that most closely meets your requirements, but you will also have a thorough understanding of the subject matter and what to expect of the project. When the time comes to hire a contractor, you will know what questions to ask, and you will be in a better position to judge quality. An educated consumer is much more likely to get a good pool at a fair price than a homeowner who relies totally on the contractor to make all of the decisions. In this chapter, you'll see many examples of pools, both above- and in-ground, and the different types of materials used to build them—concrete, vinyl, and fiberglass. There's also information you'll find useful regarding the various kinds of spas, swim spas, and hot tubs that are on the market, and the installation considerations that pertain to them.

IN-GROUND POOLS

As the name implies, an in-ground pool is set into the ground. A hole is dug and is finished, usually with concrete, vinyl, or fiberglass. Each material has its own benefits and uses; a variety of shapes is possible with an in-ground pool.

Concrete

When most people think of an in-ground pool, they think of a concrete one. This is supported by numbers from The Association of Pool and Spa Professionals (APSP), a trade group for the industry, which estimates that about 65 to 70 percent of the pools built each year are made of concrete. Those numbers come from a survey of the group's members, and although they may be a little on the high side (not all pool companies are members), there is little doubt that concrete is a popular material for pools.

Advances in concrete materials and the techniques for applying it have helped the material retain its popularity. Few, if any, professionally installed pools are poured or built with concrete block anymore. Pouring refers to building wooden forms that establish the shape of the

pool, pouring wet concrete into the forms, and removing the wood after the concrete hardens. Today, installers build concrete pools by spraying either *gunite* or *shotcrete* onto a steel-reinforced form.

Both gunite and shotcrete are cementitious materials. Although gunite is the more widely used of the two materials, both are considered equal in strength. It's only the mixing process that differentiates gunite from shotcrete. When applying gunite, the installer uses a hose that mixes the material with water. Shotcrete is delivered to the site already wet; then it is mixed with air during application. For the sake of clarity, here the term gunite will refer to both materials.

To build a gunite pool, the contractor installs steel bars, called rebar, around the sides and bottom of the excavation to create a mold for the pool's shape and to reinforce the concrete. That means the contractor can create just about any shape of pool you want. In cold climates, the walls and floor of a gunite pool should be about 9 inches thick. The top of the sides of the pool is called the bond beam because it bonds to the ground-level deck. It should be about 12 inches thick and will extend down about 18 inches. There isn't as much freezing and thawing of the soil around pools in warm climates, and therefore less stress on the gunite, so the shells of these pools should be no less than 6 inches thick.

Once the gunite cures, the installer will apply plaster over it. Plaster is similar in makeup to gunite, so the materials bond easily. Plasters are available in a variety of colors. Another option is a textured surface made of aggregate and epoxy. Perhaps the most popular choice is a plaster floor and walls topped by a few rows of ceramic tile.

A gunite pool takes two to three weeks to build. Most contractors will stipulate 30 dry working days for the project.

Smart Tip

Discuss the options with your pool builder, and be sure to ask how the finish color and texture will affect the pool when it is filled with water. For example, plain white plaster makes the water in a pool take on a bluish cast.—

2

Diving In

Accentuate a concrete pool, left, with tile, and a distinctive patio, such as the one shown here.

A free-form in-ground pool, right, makes the most of this natural setting.

Vinyl

When people talk about a vinyl in-ground pool they are referring to the liner material. Products vary from one pool manufacturer to another, but basically a vinyl pool consists of the liner and wall panels, which can be constructed of aluminum, galvanized steel, plastic, or pressure-treated plywood. Each company has its own method for anchoring the walls. To support the liner on the floor of the pool, some contractors pour a thin concrete pad while others use a sand base.

These pools are packaged systems. The manufacturer has probably honed and refined the design over the years. And if the installer has worked in the past with the product you select, there should not be any problem with the installation. For most vinyl in-ground pools, the installer does need to backfill the area behind the panels while the pool is filling with water so that the pressure on both sides of the panel remains equal. An experienced crew should be able to install a vinyl pool in about one week.

Unlike gunite pools, vinyl pools come in a finite number of shapes—but there are dozens available. And what they lack in choice of shapes they certainly make up in liner designs. The number of liner patterns is endless; most companies offer dozens. You can find everything from solid colors to designs resembling ceramic tile or even round river rock. If you so desired, you could have your initials printed on the liner. The liners themselves are usually 20 to 27 millimeters thick and will last about 10 to 15 years.

Vinyl pools used to be an inexpensive alternative to gunite pools. But because vinyl is a petroleum-based product, an increase in the cost of petroleum may signal an increase in the cost of vinyl pool liners.

Fiberglass

A fiberglass pool arrives at your house in one monolithic shell—sort of like a big tub on a flatbed truck. This is the complete pool shell, including cutouts for the drain, skimmer, and returns. While this does limit your choice of sizes and shapes, you will still find plenty fiberglass pools from which to choose. One manufacturer offers over 40 different pools, including some that have deep sections for diving.

Actually, fiberglass is the reinforcing material used in this type of pool. The inside surface of the pool is a gel coat to which the fiberglass has been laminated. A fiberglass pool costs about 10 percent more than a comparable gunite pool, and shipping costs can drive the price up even more. In addition, it may not be available in some areas. But the typical $1/2$- to $3/8$-inch walls are slick and smooth and discourage algae growth, thereby cutting down on maintenance and saving on the use of pool chemicals. Once the pool is on site, a crew can install it in about one week.

Hybrid System. At least one manufacturer offers what it calls a Uniwall system. Here fiberglass panel walls are rolled into the excavation. The panels are only about 4 feet tall, however, so the lower walls of pools that are more than 4 feet deep are made of concrete.

A vinyl pool, opposite, can come in one of many liner designs and colors.

A fiberglass pool, right, comes as a one-piece shell, but you can add accessories, such as a diving board.

ABOVEGROUND POOLS

When it comes to aboveground, or on-ground, pools, there are a variety of products from which to choose, including rectangular, round, and oval shapes; small, shallow, child-size pools; large pools that are usually 48 to 52 inches deep; and even custom-sized models. The pools consist of vinyl liners supported by steel, aluminum, or resin walls. In general, prices range from about $1,500 to close to $20,000.

Aboveground pools offer numerous advantages, the most obvious of which is the speed of installation. You can get the notion to buy a pool on a Monday and host a pool party by the weekend. Some preparation work should be performed before installing this type of pool, but it is minimal compared with what's involved with any of the in-ground installations.

The higher-end aboveground pools are those that have attached decking systems. These systems range from a small platform at one end of the pool to decks that totally surround the swimming area with space at one end for chaise lounges and dining tables. Some pools come with the decking systems, or you can add your own. Adding decks, fencing, and landscaping turns the pool into a complete recreation area that can also be an attractive focal point in the yard.

Although aboveground pools should be installed on a level spot, the condition of the soil itself usually isn't a concern. The same is true if there's a high water table or poor subsurface drainage. As long as there is a firm base below the pool, it should be fine.

Although nothing takes the place of full-time adult supervision of children using a pool, it is possible to make a case in favor of an aboveground pool based on safety. Aboveground pools are usually 4 or 4½ feet deep—a good depth for pool games but not so deep that an adult or even an older child couldn't reach a small child in trouble quickly and easily. And because the pool sits on the ground, the chances of someone accidentally falling in the water are cut dramatically. Even access to a pool surrounded by a deck can be greatly reduced by installing a gate that locks at the bottom of the deck's stairway that leads up to the swimming area.

SPAS AND HOT TUBS

When compared with full-size swimming pools, spas and hot tubs seem to come in an endless variety of sizes and designs. For the sake of clarity, we will use the term "hot tub" to refer to the classic, aboveground round wooden tub that is outfitted with benches and may or may not have jets for stirring up the water. Here, "spas" will refer to any in-ground or aboveground vessel that has built-in benches for seating and jets to agitate the water and relax and soothe tired muscles.

In-Ground Spas

Many in-ground spas are installed at the same time as an in-ground swimming pool. Pool dealers who sell concrete pools may even include a matching spa as part of the installation. In most cases, these spas are located within easy reach of the main pool, usually right next to it. Other options include acrylic, thermoplastic, stainless-steel, and fiberglass in-ground spas. Finishes range from the smooth coatings on acrylic spas to ceramic tiles on steel or fiberglass shells.

As with swimming pools, the spa's circulation system is usually located away from the spa itself. That is one of the reasons in-ground spas are often part of a larger swimming-pool project. It is less expensive and easier on the nerves to dig up your yard only once to bury the necessary piping.

In-ground spas have a low profile look that many people prefer. But if you are putting in a spa without a pool, consider an in-ground model carefully. These spas require excavation and trenching while aboveground models don't, although there are some installation requirements. If the new spa

An aboveground pool with a deck, opposite, utilizes a limited backyard area.

A fiberglass spa, above right, can be combined with a large pool.

Tile decking, right, looks terrific surrounding a custom-built spa and pool.

is part of the pool project, make sure that the circulation system can handle the requirements of both a pool and a spa. Often the pool and spa share a common filtration system and heater. Spas have different sanitation, water movement, and heat requirements than pools. A circulation system dedicated to the pool—and another one for the spa—will ensure the proper water quality for both.

Aboveground Spas

Also called portable spas, the typical model includes an acrylic, fiberglass, or thermoplastic shell and skirting to surround the shell. Between the tub itself and the exterior cladding are all the piping, filters, heaters, and controls.

Size. Portable spas range in size from models that can hold two people to those that can seat up to eight. A large model can easily measure 7 x 9 feet, but because it is only about 3 feet high, delivery people can turn the spa on its side to get it through most doorways and openings.

The larger the size of the spa, the more expensive it is. A bigger spa means more jets, more plumbing, and bigger heaters and filters to service a larger amount of water. An empty 7- x 9-foot spa can weigh up to 1,000 pounds. Fill it, and it could easily weigh 5,500 pounds.

Jets. Premium spas might contain 20, 30, or over 40 jets, depending on the size of the shell. Better companies provide a number of different types of jets. They all mix air with water under pressure, but the size and type of jet can create different effects. Some jets are specially designed and located for back muscles, others provide a vigorous foot massage, and so on. Look for adjustable jets where they will do you the most good. Sit in a spa to see how it feels before you buy it.

Finish. Acrylic shells are the most common. Look for a smooth, even finish. Some of the new plastics are solid color all the way through the material.

Pumps and Filters. Buying a portable spa means that there is no worrying about sizing pumps and filters. Better

Smart Tip

Insulated spas tend to be less noisy than uninsulated models. The insulation also holds the pipes and other equipment in place during shipping.—D.S.

spas have multiple pumps—one dedicated to the filtration system and one, sometimes two, dedicated to the jets. Portable spas usually have cartridge-type filters the size of which will vary with the size of the spa. With spa filters, bigger is better. Consider filter area when comparing one model against another.

Insulation. Energy-efficient spas are built with foam insulation around the shell. Most of the cost of running a spa can be attributed to the spa's heater, so insulation is an important consideration in many parts of the country. All spas should have covers.

Controls. Most controls are mounted right on the top of the shell. Those that are covered when the spa's cover is in place cannot be turned on accidentally. Top-of-the-line models have electronic programmable controls.

A portable spa in a sunroom, above, allows you to enjoy every season of the year.

A circular aboveground spa, above right, can be installed indoors or outdoors.

A secluded backyard, right, is a great setting for an outdoor spa on a deck.

Spa-Installation Considerations

As mentioned, the pumps, filters, and heaters for in-ground spas are located away from the spa itself, so a certain amount of excavation and trenching is necessary. Aboveground spas are self-contained, so excavation usually isn't necessary, but there are other requirements.

A spa needs a flat, level surface that can support its weight, the weight of the water, and the people in the spa. This is probably too much for the average backyard deck to hold. Discuss with your dealer where you plan on placing the spa; he can recommend any necessary support construction. If you plan to locate the spa at ground level, many manufacturers recommend installing the spa on a 4-inch-thick reinforced-concrete pad.

Smaller models run on a 20-amp, 120-volt electrical service. In fact, you can plug them into an existing outlet pro-

tected by a ground-fault circuit interrupter (GFCI). All modern spas are equipped with their own GFCI plugs. In many cases, a 20-amp circuit cannot provide power for the spa's pumps and heater simultaneously. This usually isn't a problem if the spa is small. However, large models need enough power to run the heater and the pumps at the same time. Bigger spas usually require 50-amp, 220-volt service and are hardwired—a job for an experienced electrician.

Hot Tubs

Hot tubs captured the imagination of the country during the 1970s. The spa industry was nothing like it is today, so to many people the idea of sitting in a tub of hot water to relax was a very "California" thing to do. Today, hot tubs are often casually lumped together with the types of spas discussed above, but they are not the same.

A classic hot tub is made of wood. Typically it's redwood or cedar because the heartwood of these trees is naturally resistant to decay and insects. Wood also provides a tactile experience in a hot tub that you can't find with acrylic or some other man-made material. Hot tubs are put together the way barrels or casks are assembled. The vertical wood staves have beveled edges that allow each stave to fit into the next. Iron hoops encircle the tub. When the hoops are tightened, the staves are pressed together tightly. Fill the tub with water and the wood absorbs moisture, swells, and forms a watertight seal. Add some benches and plumbing, and you have a hot tub.

Some early hot-tub users experienced problems, usually with leaks or sanitation. Some hot tubs were poorly made, but many owners didn't realize that hot tubs, like

An elaborate tropical backyard, left, is the perfect place to have a large spa installed with your pool.

A traditional hot tub, below, transforms a wooden deck or patio into a relaxing getaway.

spas, require a strict maintenance schedule. A lack of maintenance not only made the water dirty, it also corroded or otherwise damaged the wood or equipment. If you decide on a traditional hot tub, it is important to adhere to the manufacturer's maintenance recommendations. Also be sure to follow its directions regarding filling and draining the tubs. Leaving a tub empty for more than a few days causes the wood to shrink, leading to leaks when you fill it later.

Buying a Spa or Hot Tub

Try out a spa before you buy it. Many dealers have filled display models in their showrooms for you to do just that. Plan ahead of time, and wear a bathing suit under your clothes so that you can jump in and see how different models "fit." At the very least, climb into an empty spa to see how it feels. Move around to the different areas. Premium spas have a number of different seating arrangements. Would you and the people who will usually be enjoying the spa be comfortable in the different seats? Are the jets placed where they will do you the most good? Consider the depth. Will everyone who uses the spa be able to keep his or her head above water when seated?

Check the warranties. Manufacturers usually provide separate warranties for the finish, cabinet, and equipment. These vary, but 5 years on the finish and cabinet and 1 to 3 years on the pumps and filters is about standard. There are various types of warranties available, so it pays to shop around for the best one.

Perhaps more important than the warranty is the level of service you can expect from the dealer. A dealer with an established reputation who has experience selling, servicing, and repairing spas from a variety of manufacturers will most likely be a good source of information and help if something should go wrong once the spa or hot tub is installed.

This indoor spa overlooks an adjacent outdoor pool area.

Swim Spas

A swim spa is equipped to move water to produce a counter current against which you can swim. It allows you to literally swim in place. You can use a swim spa for aerobic exercise, jogging, and hydrotherapy.

There are three ways to produce the current: a propeller system, jets, or a paddle wheel. They all offer slightly different experiences, so shop around. But perhaps more important than how the pool produces the current is the degree to which you can adjust it. You'll want a system you are comfortable with as a beginning swim-spa user and as someone looking for a challenge as you grow in strength.

Models are available for in-ground or aboveground installation. The typical swim spa is 14 or 15 feet long, about 6 or 7 feet wide, and about 3 to 6 feet deep. Most models are made of acrylic, fiberglass, or stainless steel with a vinyl liner. Their compact size means you can install a swim spa in a small yard or a room. Many models feature a separate section or seating at one end, so that you can convert the unit to a traditional spa if you like. As with portable spas, these products include the shell, pumps, filters, and heaters in one unit.

Smart Tip

Turn any regular pool into a swim spa by using a portable water-propulsion unit. Built to hang over the side of the pool, most models simply plug into any GFCI-protected outlet.—D.S.

An outdoor swim spa can be customized to fit your specific needs and design interests.

THE HEALING POWERS OF WATER

WE ALL KNOW that it feels good to sit in the warm waters of a bubbling spa, but did you ever wonder why? The typical spa is heated to about 104 degrees Fahrenheit, and according to the APSP, water that warm not only relaxes muscles but also causes the blood vessels to dilate, lowering blood pressure. The buoyancy of water counteracts gravity, so sitting submerged to your shoulders can make your heart 10 to 20 percent more efficient. Buoyancy also reduces the strain on muscles and joints. Add to that those hydro jets designed to massage your neck, back, and feet, and you are in for one pleasurable and possibly therapeutic session.

But not everyone should use a spa. Pregnant women and people with heart disease or high or low blood pressure should consult their doctor before using a spa.

Installing a railing adds a safety feature to a therapeutic in-ground spa.

2

Diving In

INDOOR POOLS AND SPAS

For the most part, the design and construction requirements for indoor pools and spas are similar to those used for outdoor models. But there are a few important differences that are worth noting.

Any enclosed structure that contains a pool or a large spa needs adequate ventilation to remove the large amounts of moisture-laden air these installations produce. Inadequate ventilation could lead to damaged building components, rust forming on metal elements, and respiratory concerns for some people. Your builder can brief you on local ventilation requirements.

Gas and oil heaters must be vented to the outdoors. While venting heating equipment usually isn't an issue in outdoor installations, indoor pool and spa heaters have the same requirements as your home's heating system.

POOL AND SPA PLUMBING

There are many reasons why more homeowners than ever are considering pools and spas, but perhaps none are more important than the almost universal use of polyvinyl chloride (PVC) piping. This plastic piping is less expensive and easier to work with than copper piping. But more importantly, a pool contractor does not need someone on his crew who knows how to solder fittings. Sections of piping can be joined together quickly and easily by applying special glue to the pipe ends. With just a little practice, almost anyone can learn to join two pieces of plastic pipe together.

For the homeowner, the advantage of using PVC piping lies in the fact that it does a better job than copper does in resisting the caustic chemicals used in pools. PVC materials will last for years, and the type used in pools, Schedule 40, can be buried without damaging the pipe. In addition, if there is an emergency and you have to replace a section of pipe, you can do it with the materials you find at the local home center.

Working with PVC Piping

Pool piping is generally 1½ or 2 inches in diameter. That is the inside diameter of the pipe, the part that actually carries the water. It is sold in straight lengths and a variety of fittings, such as 45- and 90-degree fittings for making turns and T-fittings for joining branch lines to main lines. There are couplings for joining straight runs together, and reducers for connecting pipes of unequal diameters to one another.

Most PVC is joined together by a chemical reaction created when you apply solvent cement to the pipe ends. When someone has to join two sections of pipe, the solvent cement melts the plastic just enough to fuse the two surfaces together. The joint winds up stronger than the

This custom pool, left, was designed to fit a sloped site.

A fountain spilling into a pool, opposite, hides piping and accessorizes a wall.

pipe. Some fittings have threads for joining pipe. In this case, plumber's tape, not solvent cement, is used to form a strong union.

Problems with PVC. Despite its many advantages, PVC piping does have some weak points. For one, sunlight can weaken it over time. Some manufacturers add inhibitors to the formula to help the pipe resist the ultraviolet rays of the sun. Many simply suggest that you paint any exposed pipe to protect it from the sun.

PVC piping is not made to carry very hot water. Most of the water used in a pool or spa falls within the safety range of the piping, but there could be a problem in the areas where heated water first flows from the heater. In those cases, manufacturers specify installing a short length of cast-iron pipe directly at the heater. Within that length, enough excess heat will dissipate through the walls of the metal pipe so that it will be safe to use PVC to continue the pipe run.

pools and spas

design ideas for

This vanishing-edge pool, right, enhances the magnificent view from this hilltop patio. Note the cantilevered seating area.

Exercise becomes a pleasure when your lap pool is part of a well-designed landscape, such as the one shown below.

A waterfall effect, opposite top, adds a unique dimension to the concrete deck surrounding this pool.

Plan the pool, opposite bottom, pool house, and landscaping to work together as a unified design to achieve the best results.

pools and spas

design ideas for

Waterfalls, opposite top, are not only a unique way to fill your pool or spa, the sound adds to your overall enjoyment.

Pools are great, but why settle for just a pool when it can be the centerpiece of a complete outdoor living area, opposite bottom.

This structure, left, gives new meaning to the term pool house. Indoor pools provide year-round enjoyment.

Enjoy the nighttime, below, by incorporating pool and landscape lighting into your plans.

pools and spas

design ideas for

In-ground spas, opposite top, are usually built when the pool is constructed. The stone coping adds a rustic touch to the design.

Is this an in-ground or above-ground pool, opposite bottom, This retaining wall is a solution for a sloping yard.

Down the hill and through the woods to the spa we go, above. Include nature in your designs.

Be sure to provide natural light, left, and plenty of ventilation for your indoor pool.

CHAPTER 3

POOL AND SPA EQUIPMENT

Pool Gear

As you begin enjoying your new pool, you will come to realize that none of the fun would be possible without the equipment and components that run behind the scenes. The water in large above-ground and in-ground pools—the ones covered in this book—must be cleaned and, in many cases, heated for your maximum enjoyment and safety. To accomplish this, a pump powers a circulation system and draws water from the pool, moves it through a filter, into a heater, and then back into the pool. (To see how this works, refer to "The Pool and Spa Circulation System," on page 62.) The circulation system is the first of a two-part scheme for keeping your pool and spa water sparkling clean. The second part involves using chemicals and other methods to remove harmful bacteria and other impurities, a topic that is covered in Chapter 5, "Sparkling Water—Pool Chemistry Made Easy," which begins on page 94. In this chapter, you will learn how the skimmers, pumps, filters, heaters, and pool and spa covers help in maintaining clean, healthy water. You'll also find out what is involved in selecting the right-size heaters and pumps, and which ones are more expensive to operate and why. Plus, there are tips for keeping down costs and conserving energy. None of this information is very complicated, and it will be useful.

SKIMMERS, DRAINS, AND INLETS

Skimmers, drains, and inlets are the beginning and end points of the pool's circulation system. Skimmers and the main drain work together to get water from the pool to the pump and filtration system, which are discussed later. Inlets are the reentry points for the water after it has been filtered and, in some cases, heated.

Skimmers are usually built into the side of in-ground pools just below the coping. Aboveground pools may have skimmers that hang over the side of the pool.

Skimmers consist of a basket, a floating gatelike device called a *weir*, and plumbing that connects the skimmer to the pool's pump. As the name states, they are designed to skim the surface of any floating debris, such as leaves, grass clippings, or other objects. As the pool's pump pulls

THE POOL AND SPA CIRCULATION SYSTEM

The pool and spa circulation system begins at the skimmers and main drain. The pump, which is the heart of the circulation system, pulls water from these areas and then pushes it to the filter's heater (if there is one), and any other equipment in the system. The clean water then returns to the pool or spa through the inlets.

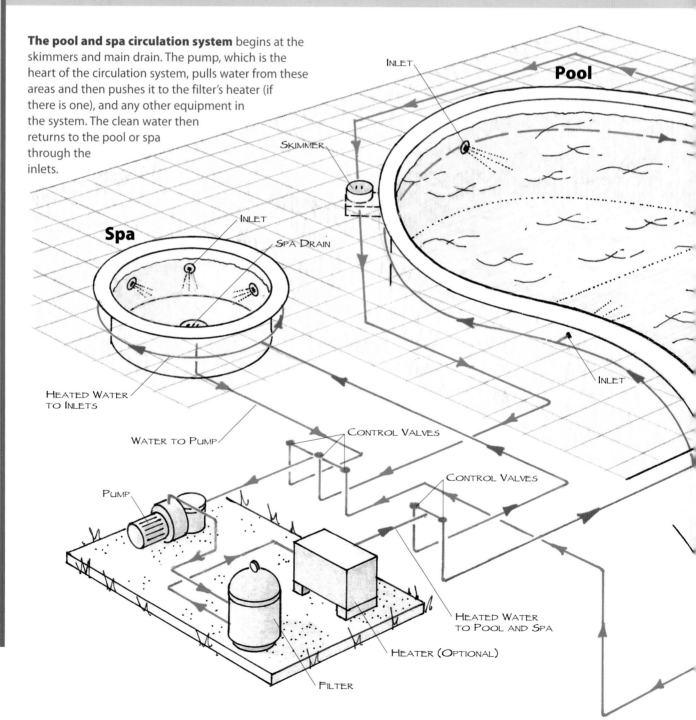

Pool

INLET

SKIMMER

Spa

INLET

SPA DRAIN

HEATED WATER TO INLETS

INLET

WATER TO PUMP

CONTROL VALVES

CONTROL VALVES

PUMP

HEATED WATER TO POOL AND SPA

HEATER (OPTIONAL)

FILTER

water through the system, the weir drops to let in anything floating on the surface of the water. When the pump is switched off, the weir returns to a vertical position so as not to release anything that is in the skimmer cavity. The basket keeps material from going to the pump and filter. You can reach it through an access hatch in the pool deck. Debris that blocks the flow of water makes the pump work harder, so clean the basket daily.

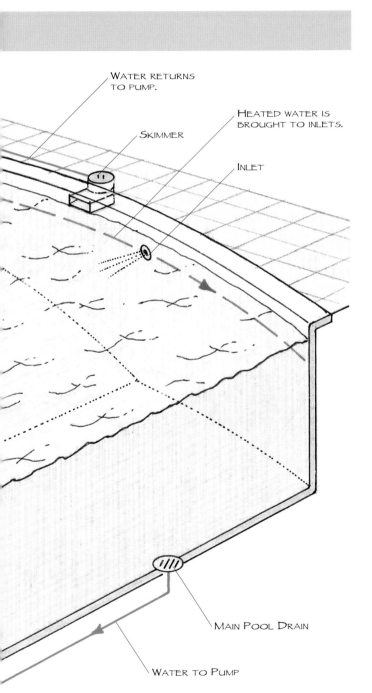

WATER RETURNS TO PUMP.

HEATED WATER IS BROUGHT TO INLETS.

SKIMMER

INLET

MAIN POOL DRAIN

WATER TO PUMP

A skimmer basket, located within the pool deck, above, is easy to access.

An in-ground skimmer, below, is located in the side of the pool and catches leaves and other debris.

THE HYDROSTATIC VALVE

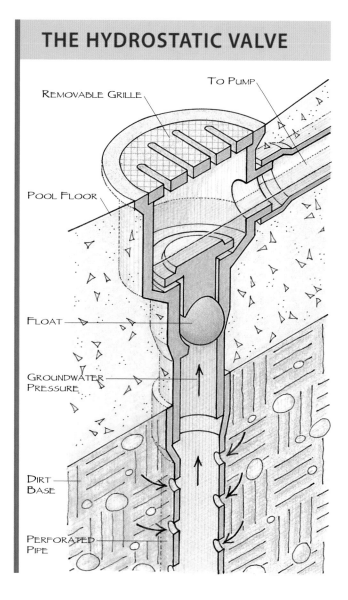

REMOVABLE GRILLE

TO PUMP

POOL FLOOR

FLOAT

GROUNDWATER PRESSURE

DIRT BASE

PERFORATED PIPE

The plumbing for some skimmers is connected to the plumbing from the main drain. A diverter valve allows you to adjust the suction for each. Another type has an equalizer line, which is a 12- to 18-inch section of pipe that connects the bottom of the skimmer to an opening in the side of the pool well below normal water level. The reason for both is that if the pool's water level should drop below the skimmer, the pump can still pull water to prevent air from entering the system.

Plan on installing one skimmer for every 500 square feet of pool surface. Skimmers also provide a connection for pool vacuums.

Main Drain

The main drain at the bottom of the pool is connected to the pump. The grate on many drains conceals a port that runs to the pump, and also a hydrostatic or pressure-relief valve. This valve is designed to relieve pressure created by ground water under the pool.

For safety, main drain lines should contain a Safety Vacuum Release System. This system automatically cuts power should a swimmer or wader become stuck to a drain due to its suction. Discuss this option with your pool builder.

Inlets. Inlets direct water back into the pool. Some inlets are adjustable. This is important because inlets aid the distribution of any chemicals added to pool water through the circulation system.

An adjustable inlet next to the stairs allows you to change the direction of the water flowing into your pool.

PUMPS

Pools require centrifugal pumps to keep the water moving through the system. As shown in the illustration on page 62, pool water enters through the inlet—pool installers call it an *influent line*. The water first flows into a strainer basket that catches any large debris such as leaves or grass clippings. The basket should remove anything that might clog or damage the pump. The heart of the pump is the *impeller*, which is a circular disk with raised vanes that spins to create centrifugal force. The spinning of the impeller, along with the design of the chamber, called the *volute*, that houses the impeller, creates the pulling or sucking action of the pump. From the volute, the impeller directs the water up through the top of the pump housing to an *effluent line* and on to the pool's filter.

There are two impeller designs used in pools pumps: *closed-face* and *semi-open-face* impellers.

Closed-Face Impeller. This device has two plates with vanes in between them. Water is forced in through a hole in the center and then thrown out at the end of each vane. Closed-face models are very efficient at moving water. But any material that gets past the strainer basket can clog up the impeller.

Semi-Open-Face Impeller. This type of impeller has a flat plate with slots. It will pulverize any debris and tends to be easier to maintain than the closed-face version.

Modern pool and spa pumps are self-priming, meaning they automatically expel air from the system when the pump is turned on. If the pump on your pool wasn't self-priming and you didn't remove the air from the system, the pump would not be able to pull the water and the motor could be damaged. Pool pumps range in power from 0.5 to up to 3 horsepower. They are also rated for continuous duty, which means the pump is designed to run 24 hours a day.

There are single-speed and two-speed pumps. Two-speed pumps are becoming more popular because their motors run at a low speed—about 1,750 revolutions per minute (rpm)—for routine pumping but then increase to high speed—about 3,450 rpm—when a lot of people are using the pool at the same time. Most spas have two-speed pumps. The lower speed pulls the water through the filtration system, and the higher speed operates the jets.

Sizing the Pump

Your pool dealer will recommend a certain pump for your pool and circulation system. He will base his decision on the capacity of your pool in gallons of water (see "Calculating Pool Capacity," on page 80) and the desired *flow rate*, or the amount of water that should flow through the pump. To find it, you will have to determine the turnover time, which is how often all of the water in the pool should be circulated through the system. Recommended turnover times vary, but eight hours is about average. So if you want the pool water to go through the circulation system every eight hours, divide the pool's capacity by 8 to find the flow rate in gallons per hour (capacity/turnover rate in hours = flow rate per hour).

For example, in a pool that holds 16,875 gallons of water, the equation would be:

16,875/8 = 2,109 (approximately)

To find the flow rate in gallons per minute, divide that number by 60. For example:

2,109/60 = 35.15 gallons per minute

The next step involves determining the amount of resistance in the circulation system. This is called *total dynamic head* or *head loss*. Everything in the circulation system resists the flow of water and makes the pump work harder. Even the smooth inside surfaces of the PVC pipe offers some resistance to the flow of water. Your contractor will make this calculation. A good contractor will

Smart Tip

It Doesn't Add Up. One way to calculate head loss is to convert the resistance offered by valves and fittings to an equivalent length of straight pipe. But there's a little quirk in measuring resistance.

A 90-degree elbow on a 2-inch pipe equals the resistance of 8.6 feet of straight 2-inch pipe. A 45-degree elbow on a 2-inch pipe equals the resistance of 2.8 feet of straight 2-inch pipe. The 90-degree elbow has over three times the resistance of a 45-degree elbow, rather than two times the resistance that logic would indicate. There may be times when using two 45-degree elbows makes better sense.—D.S.

A pump curve chart, right, is used by the manufacturer to help homeowners buy the right pump for their individual and specific pool needs.

try to come up with ways to limit head loss. (See the Smart Tip on page 65.)

Pump manufacturers print pump curves (see the illustration, "Pump Performance Curves," right) for their products so that you and your contractor can match the right pump to your needs. To use the curve, find the head loss on the vertical axis, and draw a horizontal line. Then find the flow rate in gallons per minute on the horizontal axis, and draw a vertical line up through the chart. The intersection of the two lines indicates the pump that is best for you. When the line falls between two curves, choose the higher, more powerful pump. You will compensate for any errors made in calculating head loss, and the cost difference between pumps is minimal, about $100 between a 1- and 2-horsepower pump.

As the homeowner, there are a few other things to consider in pump selection. For one, the strainer basket needs to be cleaned on a regular basis. A pump with a clear plastic cover over the basket allows you to check the condition of the basket at a glance. The lid itself should be easy to remove and replace.

FILTERS

If you review the illustration on page 62, you'll see that the pool's filter is located downstream of the pump. The filter's job is to remove dirt from the pool water. Actually, the cleaning process starts at the strainer basket that is attached to the pump. But the basket catches only large items such as leaves or branches. For the stuff that makes water cloudy, much of which you can't even see with the naked eye, you need a pool filter.

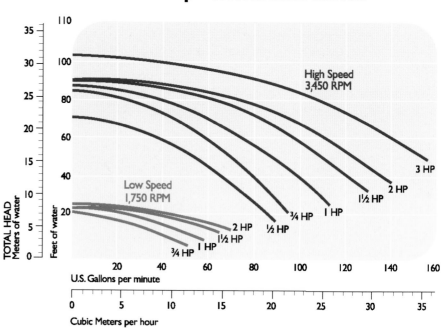

Pump Performance Curves

It's important to remember that a filter is only one-half of the cleaning system. No filter is fine enough to catch and remove bacteria from the water. For that you need to sanitize the water using chlorine or some other chemical, as discussed in Chapter 5.

There are three types of filters that are used in residential pools: *cartridge filters, diatomaceous earth filters, and sand filters.* They all do a good job of removing impurities from water.

Smart Tip

There may be small differences in cost for filters, but it pays to compare because manufacturers often offer specials. Your pool dealer or contractor will definitely have an opinion on which type of filter to install. But they all work differently and have different maintenance requirements of which you should be aware before you make a final decision.—D.S.

Be sure to maintain your pool's cleaning system on a regular basis so that the water is clean and refreshing for the entire swimming season, opposite.

Cartridge Filters

Cartridge filters have been around for some time, but they seem to be gaining in popularity in many parts of the country. They consist of a tank that houses three or four cylindrical filtering elements. The filters are actually made of polyester or some other material that can provide a superfine filtering surface. The fabric catches and holds the impurities until you clean or replace the filter.

The cartridges can filter out anything down to about 5 to 10 microns in size. A grain of table salt is about 90 microns; anything below about 35 microns is invisible to the naked eye. It is important to remember that with any filter, a small amount of dirt actually aids the filtering process. In other words, a filter becomes more efficient the longer it operates. However, there is a point at which the filter is holding onto too much dirt and must be replaced. (See Chapter 7, "Pool Keeping—Routine Maintenance and Care," beginning on page 136, for more information.)

In most areas, cartridge filters are less expensive than diatomaceous earth filters but cost more than sand filters. However, cartridge filters are popular because of the minimal maintenance involved. Some families will find it sufficient to simply hose off the cartridges a few times during the swimming season to keep them working properly. Others may need to soak the filters in detergent or replace them. In any case, maintenance takes only a few minutes to keep the filtration system in top shape. Most portable spas contain cartridge filters.

POOL FILTER ANATOMY

Cartridge Filter

DE Filter

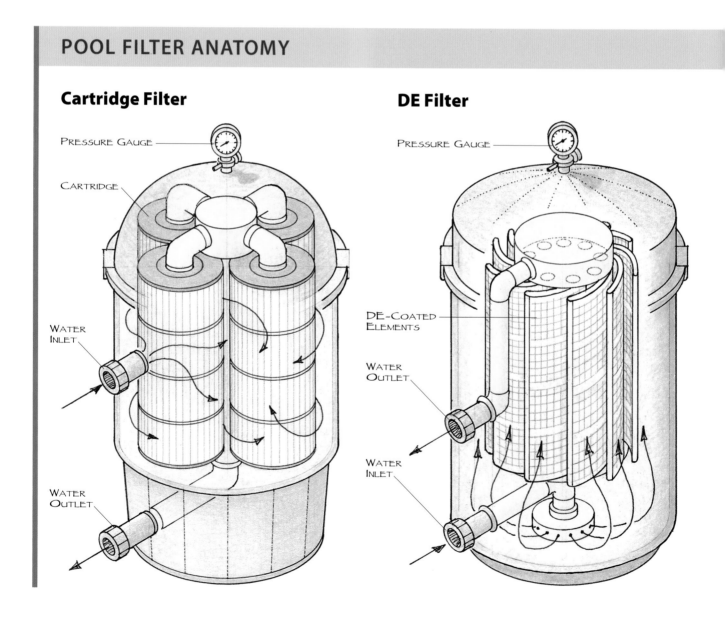

Diatomaceous Earth Filters

Called DE filters, these products can filter out dirt as small as 3 to 5 microns. If you opened the tank of a DE filter it would look somewhat similar to a cartridge filter. But the grids are packed with diatomaceous earth, a powder made up of billions of fossilized plankton skeletons. It is this powder that actually catches and holds the dirt.

DE filters are usually the most expensive type, and they get the water cleaner than the other filters. But the necessary maintenance can be a drawback for some homeowners. Most manufacturers call for backwashing to clean the filter. In backwashing, the system reverses the flow of water. The clean water cleanses the filter. The dirty water is then drained from the system.

However, you'll find many pool service technicians who say that backwashing alone usually isn't sufficient for DE filters. Water takes the path of least resistance, so if there is a channel or hole in the DE pack on the grids, the water will flow through openings in the filter cake and leave the rest of the filter dirty. To really clean a DE filter, you must remove the grids and clean off the spent DE. This presents the problem of what to do with the old DE. Many towns will not allow you to simply dump it down the sewer. Some places classify it as a hazardous waste that requires special handling. Be sure to check local ordinances before deciding on a DE filter.

Sand Filters

These filters use—you guessed it—sand as the filtering medium. Sand filters look like large balls and they can hold hundreds of pounds of pool-grade sand. Basically, water flows into the top of the filer housing and makes its way down through the sand bed where the sharp edges of the sand catch the dirt. On a micron-to-micron comparison, sand filters remove the least amount of dirt—particles as small as about 20 to 25 microns. But again, for a time, the dirt left behind contributes to the filtering process. Sand filters certainly are efficient enough to keep just about any pool clean.

To keep a sand filter working, you must clean it as often as once a week during swimming season. Maintenance means backwashing where the flow of clean water is reversed back into the filter. The problem with this, however, is that the backwashed water is simply wasted. A typical backwashing session can waste a few hundred gallons of water—water that must be replaced in the pool. Sand filters may not be a good idea in areas that are often under water restrictions.

Sizing Filters

As with sizing a pump, you will need to know the capacity of the pool. (See "Calculating Pool Capacity," on page 80.) You will also have to calculate the flow rate. This is a measurement of the amount of water that should flow through the filter. To find it, you or your pool dealer will need to determine how often all of the water in the pool should be circulated. This exercise is the same as the one explained in "Sizing the Pump," on page 65.

Sand Filter

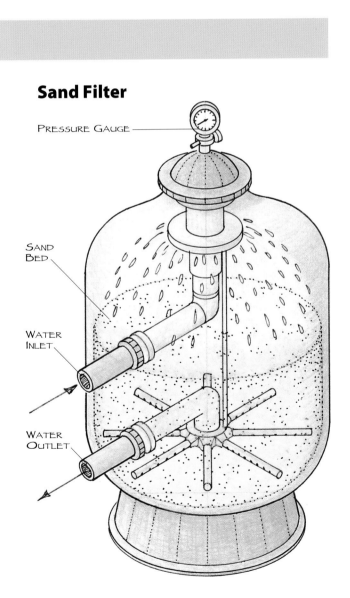

PRESSURE GAUGE

SAND BED

WATER INLET

WATER OUTLET

3

Pool Gear

Let's assume that you want all of the water in the pool to be circulated through the filter system in eight hours, an average circulation rate. Divide the pool's capacity by 8 to find the flow rate in gallons per hour (capacity/turnover rate in hours = flow rate per hour). For example, for a pool that holds 16,875 gallons of water, the equation would be:

16,875/8 = 2,109 (approximately)

That is the number of gallons that should flow through the filter per hour. Divide that number by 60 to find the flow rate in gallons per minute.

2,109/60 = 35.15 gallons per minute

Once you have the flow rate that you need to keep the pool clean, in this case 35.15 gallons per minute, you can look for a filter that meets those requirements. To determine a filter's flow rate, multiply the square footage of fil-

Waterfalls, trees, and rocks serve as the perfect disguise for your pool circulation system.

POOL FILTERS AT A GLANCE

POOL FILTERS AT A GLANCE

Diatomaceous Earth

Cost: Most Expensive

Remarks: Although they provide the best filtration at start up, these filters must be backwashed once a week. They should be disassembled and cleaned at least two times a year. This is a messy process, and there may be local restrictions on disposing of spent DE earth.

DE FILTER

Cartridge

CARTRIDGE FILTER

Cost: Midrange

Remarks: Good for installing a large filter area in a tight spot. Cartridges require cleaning about three times per year. Cartridges should be replaced about every five years.

MULTIPORT
VALVE

Sand

Cost: Least Expensive

Remarks: Good choice for a homeowner who plans on maintaining his or her own pool. Filters require backwashing (which wastes water) about once a week, but multiport valves make this an easy process that takes about five minutes.

SAND FILTER

tering area by filter rate, which is the number of gallons that flow through 1 square foot of filter area per minute. This isn't as confusing as it sounds. Both numbers are available through the filter manufacturer. They are listed on the product's fact sheets and in some cases you can even find them on the manufacturer's Web site. So suppose you are looking for a sand filter. Manufacturer X offers one model with 1.8 square feet of filter area (that is the actual filtering medium, not the size of the tank) with a filter rate of 20 gallons per minute per square foot.

$$1.8 \times 20 = 36$$

That is pretty close to our requirement of 35.15 gallons per minute flow rate. But unfortunately, even though Brand X meets the requirements, it is too close for comfort. Common wisdom in the industry calls for oversizing filters. Remember, once the filter begins catching impurities it actually does a better job of filtering out debris. But the debris also lowers the filter's rate of flow. To compensate for this, the filter should be a little larger than indicated by the calculations. How much larger? A lot of that will depend on the swim load and how often the pool is used. Your pool dealer will be able to help you.

You can either buy a filter with a faster filter rate or one with a larger filtering area. Say you went up to a filter with 2.5 sq. ft. of area:

2.5 x 20 = 50 gallons per minute

This is a better filter for the pool. You could also find one with a faster filter rate, but the faster water flows through the filtering medium, the fewer impurities it leaves behind. It is best to chose a filter with a larger filtering area.

When making your final selection, remember that filters will require maintenance. If you are considering a DE or sand filter, you or your pool service will have to backwash it. Most newer filters are equipped with multiport valves that make backwashing as simple as turning a dial on the valve, about as close to automatic as possible. You should also make sure that it is easy to open the tank to get at cartridge filters.

Electric Resistance and Oil Heaters

These are two other types of pool heaters. Unlike heat pumps, which also use electricity, electric-resistance heat is more direct. An electric current creates heat that warms the water. These heaters are usually not a first choice for pool owners because local utility rates make them expensive to run. They are usually specified if natural gas or propane are not available.

The same is true of oil-heated appliances. They use #2 fuel oil rather than gas to heat the water.

Sizing Heaters for Pools

There are a number of variables in choosing the correct-size heater for your pool. One of the most important is how you plan on using the pool. If you will use it frequently during the swimming season, you need a heater that provides maintenance heating, which means the water temperature

Smart Tip

Cut Heating Costs. The Reduce Swimming Pool Energy Costs program of the Department of Energy offers these tips for cutting heating bills:

- Keep a thermometer in the pool. It will help you determine what water temperature is right for you.
- Mark the "comfort setting" on the thermostat dial to avoid accidental or careless overheating.
- Lower the thermostat to 70 degrees Fahrenheit if the pool will be unused for three or four days. For longer periods, shut off the heater.
- Protect the pool from wind. A 7-mile-per-hour wind at the water's surface can triple costs.
- Use a pool cover. This can reduce your pool's energy consumption by 50 to 75 percent.
- Get your pool heater tuned up annually.—D.S.

POOL HEATER SIZING TABLE

Temperature Rise (deg. F)	10	15	20	25	30
Pool surface area in square feet	Required output in British thermal units (Btu) per hour				
200	21,000	32,000	42,000	53,000	63,000
300	32,000	48,000	73,000	79,000	95,000
400	42,000	63,000	84,000	105,000	126,000
500	53,000	79,000	105,000	131,000	157,000
600	63,000	95,000	126,000	157,000	189,000
700	74,000	110,000	147,000	184,000	220,000
800	84,000	126,000	168,000	210,000	252,000
900	95,000	142,000	189,000	236,000	285,000

remains relatively constant. If you will use the pool intermittently, it might make more sense to get a unit to provide spot heating. This is an important distinction because it affects how you calculate the size heater you will need. In very general terms, pool owners usually get maintenance heating for the pool and spot heating for the spa.

For pool heaters, you have to know the total pool surface area. (See "Calculating Pool Capacity," on page 80.) Surface area is the determining factor because most heat loss will be through evaporation from the surface. The "Pool Heater Sizing Table," opposite, is a helpful tool. In addition to knowing the surface area, you will also need to know the temperature rise. To find it, first determine how warm you want the water. Most experts, including the American Red Cross, place ideal swimming temperatures in the 78- to 82-degree range. Next, find the average ambient temperature for the coldest month the pool will be open. Subtract the ambient temperature from the swimming temperature you want, and you have the temperature rise. From there you can just read across to find the required heater output in British thermal units (Btu) per hour. Most manufacturers print similar tables, except the company's model numbers usually replace the Btu listings.

Tables like these are normally based on ideal conditions,

Spa heaters have adjustable temperatures to keep you comfortable year round.

usually a pool that is only subject to a 3-mile-per-hour wind. Higher winds mean more heat loss and require a larger heater. Also, if you are in a high elevation—4,000 feet above sea level or more—you may need a special high-altitude heater. In fact, increase the heater size by 4 percent for every 1,000 feet of elevation.

Sizing Heaters for Spas

When the spa is not part of a spa pack, which contains a heater, spa heaters are sized differently. In this case, it is not the surface area that is of concern, because spas are smaller and usually covered when they're not in use so heat loss through evaporation is generally not a problem. But to get the most value from a spa, you need to heat it up quickly to the desired temperature. The maximum for a spa temperature is 104 degrees Fahrenheit.

Once you have the preset temperature and the average ambient temperature for the coldest month the spa will be used, figure the volume of the spa. (See "Calculating Pool Capacity," page 80.) Then consult a table, such as the one on page 76, to determine the proper size heater.

SPA HEATING TABLE

Heater input in Btu per hour	125,000	175,000	250,000	325,000	400,000
Spa volume in gallons	Minutes required for each 30-degree temperature rise				
200	30	21	15	12	9
300	45	32	23	17	14
400	60	43	30	23	19
500	75	54	38	29	23
600	90	64	45	35	28
700	105	75	53	40	33
800	120	86	60	46	37
900	135	96	68	52	42
1,000	150	107	75	58	47

POOL AND SPA COVERS

There are two main reasons to invest in a cover for your pool: a cover can reduce your overall pool maintenance costs, including heating and chemical use; and it could prevent a serious accident. Not all pool covers do both, but there is enough variety out there to find the cover that best suits your needs. Or it may make sense to get two covers.

Maintenance Covers

It is going to cost you a certain amount of money each season to heat and clean your pool. The right cover can help you reduce those costs.

This retractable cover can be conveniently rolled over the pool at the end of a summer day.

Pools can consume a lot of energy and, therefore, money. The U.S. Department of Energy (DOE) has determined that evaporation accounts for 70 percent of the heat loss in both outdoor and indoor pools. It takes one Btu to raise the temperature of one pound of water one degree higher. But each pound of 80-degree water that evaporates out of a pool takes 1,048 Btu of heat with it. Covering the pool can save 50 to 70 percent in heating costs. The table "How Good Are Pool Covers," on page 79, shows the cost of heating a pool with an energy-efficient heat pump with and without a pool cover. One drawback is that if you leave covers on during the day, the pool won't be able to collect as much heat from the sun. A transparent cover cuts solar absorption by 5 to 15 percent; an opaque cover by 20 to 40 percent, according to the DOE.

But energy savings is only part of the story. A cover keeps out debris that either you or your pool's cleaning system needs to remove. Covers can reduce chemical

A safety cover is a smart option for your pool, especially if you have small children or pets.

usage by 35 to 60 percent. They also conserve water by 30 to 50 percent over pools that do not have covers.

The typical maintenance cover is made of vinyl or insulated vinyl. You'll also find a clear bubble cover—resembling a thick version of bubble wrap—that is often called a solar cover. The maintenance covers tend to last longer.

The covers themselves aren't that expensive. It's the system that puts the cover on the pool and removes it that increases the cost. The simplest is a line attached to the edges of the cover that allows you to pull it into place. Some cover manufacturers sell reels that let you roll up the cover when you want to use the pool. Automatic systems, the most expensive and the most convenient, unroll and roll up the cover with a touch of a button or the turn of a key. Some of these systems cover the entire area

A spa cover helps to keep the water at a warm temperature and cuts down your energy costs.

around the edges of the pool. Others run on tracks that are recessed under the coping. The result is a cover that seems to be part of the pool itself.

It's important to know that some maintenance covers meet the requirements of The American Society for Testing and materials (ASTM) standard F1346-91 (1996) for pool safety covers. But others do not. The typical mainte-

Smart Tip

You will have to provide a space for the rolled up cover along one edge of the pool, unless you use a retractable cover. This area can be sunken into the ground and must be built when the pool is installed. Other covers can rest at ground level and be disguised as a bench.—D.S.

nance cover will not support the weight of a child if he or she should fall onto it.

Safety Covers

Although some maintenance covers are also safety covers, some aren't. A safety cover meets the requirements in ASTM F1346-91 (1996). ASTM standards require that a cover will be able to support the weight of a small child if the child should walk on the cover. There are some covers that let you drain standing water so that accumulation from rain or other sources does not become a hazard. These types of covers are made of a tough mesh material and are anchored to the pool deck with stainless-steel hardware. This is the type of cover to use over the pool in the off season.

Spa Covers

Energy efficiency is an important element of a spa. The goal is to keep the water extremely warm—100-plus degrees Fahrenheit—even though the outside temperature may be much colder. Most portable spas have insulated shells, so a spa without a cover is really a waste of money.

Spa covers should fit the top of the spa securely, allowing for any surface-mounted controls. Covers are usually secured to the side of the spa with clips and have a few inches of foam insulation to protect against heat loss.

Although unwieldy, a spa cover can usually be removed and replaced by an adult. Lifting mechanisms are available that make the job easier.

HOW GOOD ARE POOL COVERS?

THE FOLLOWING TABLE shows what it costs to heat a 1,000-sq. ft. pool in a variety of geographical locations with and without a pool cover. The table assumes that the pool is heated by an 80-percent efficient natural-gas heater at $0.50 per therm. The pool is uncovered for 8 hours a day.

Location	Season	Pool Temperature		
		78 degrees	**80 degrees**	**82 degrees**
Miami	1/1–12/31	$2,136	$2,848	$3,600
W/cover		416	584	800
Phoenix	3/1–10/31	1,384	1,776	2,216
W/cover		96	168	256
Dallas	4/1–10/31	1,512	1,920	2,456
W/cover		184	280	408
Atlanta	4/1–10/31	1,704	2,248	2,880
W/cover		320	424	592
Los Angeles	5/1–10/31	1,864	2,376	2,904
W/cover		168	304	472
Kansas City	5/1–10/31	1,434	1,872	2,384
W/cover		288	416	544
New York	5/1–9/30	1,448	1,904	2,384
W/cover		208	296	400
Chicago	5/1–9/30	1,621	2,072	2,536
W/cover		216	296	384
Denver	5/1–8/31	1,757	2,120	2,498
W/cover		123	168	243
Boston	5/31–8/31	1,712	2,096	2,504
W/cover		232	328	416
Minneapolis	6/1–9/30	1,331	1,776	2,176
W/cover		192	248	384
San Francisco	6/1–8/31	1,560	1,856	2,168
W/cover		192	320	472
Seattle	6/1–8/31	1,525	1,784	2,056
W/cover		304	424	552

Source: Reduce Swimming Pool Energy Costs program of the Department of Energy Energy Efficiency and Renewable Energy Clearinghouse

3

Pool Gear

CALCULATING POOL CAPACITY

DETERMINING pool capacity is a two-step process.

Step 1

Begin by finding the volume of the pool. To calculate the volume of any space, multiply length times width times height (l x w x h). So a rectangular pool that is 30 feet long by 15 feet wide by 5 feet deep would have a volume of 2,250 cubic feet (30 x 15 x 5 = 2,250). This is a straightforward calculation if you have a rectangular pool with a constant depth. But suppose you have a round pool? Or an oval? Or a kidney shaped pool? One of the great things about modern pools is the variety of shapes and sizes available. To help you, here are some equations to figure the volume of pools of different shapes.

Circle: radius x radius x pi (3.14) x average depth = volume

Oval: length from center point of rounded area x width from center point of rounded area x 3.14 x average depth = volume

For pools with complex shapes, break the large area down into smaller shapes. Find the volume for each section, and add them together.

Another option is to plot the shape of your pool on graph paper. Have each square represent 1 square foot of area. Count up the squares, and multiply by the average depth.

Average Depth: To find the average depth of a pool with a sloping bottom, add the depth at the shallowest end to the depth at the deepest point and then divide by two.

Step 2

Once you know the volume of your pool, calculate the number of gallons of water it holds by multiplying volume by 7.5 (approximate number of gallons of water per cubic foot). So a pool that is 2,250 cubic feet would hold about 16,875 gallons of water.

Volume x 7.5 = Total gallons

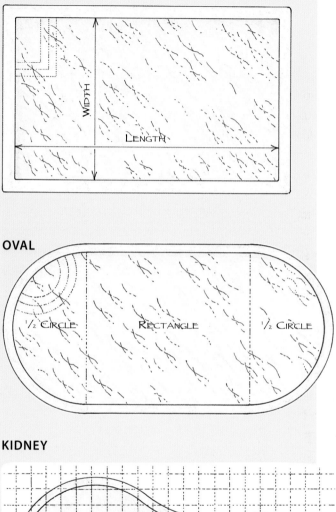

RECTANGLE

OVAL

KIDNEY

After installation is complete, beautify your pool surroundings with decorative furnishings, fences, tile patterns, and flowers, opposite.

CHAPTER 4

ACCESSORIES AND FUN STUFF

Enhancing the Experience

very pool and spa requires certain basic equipment, such as filters and pumps, to keep it clean and safe. These items and others were covered in Chapter 3, "Pool Gear—Pool and Spa Equipment," beginning on page 60. But in addition to the essentials, there are a variety of other products that can enhance your swimming or soaking experience. Some, such as diving boards and slides, simply make swimming more fun. Others—automatic pool cleaners, for example— are designed to cut down on the time and effort that is required for maintenance. Items such as pool lighting enhance the experience but have a practical side as well. This chapter will cover some of the most popular items in these categories.

Manufacturers are always introducing new products, too, so in addition to the review presented here, there may be items that you can find on a manufacturer's Web site or in the showroom. If your budget is tight, remember that you can add some of these accessories later. Ask your pool contractor or dealer for advice about what may or may not be the right choice for your setup. Find out if your friends or neighbors have recommendations about a particular product or manufacturer. Also, inquire about warranties and servicing before you buy something only to find out later that a part may take weeks to replace. Then compare prices and only purchase the best quality items you can afford.

TIMERS AND REMOTE CONTROLS

A timer, or time clock, automatically turns the equipment on and off and can be a key component to a pool or spa. With a time clock, the pump circulates water, the filter removes impurities, and the heater warms the water at preset times. So you can be sure your pool or spa is going through its normal cleaning cycle even if you are not home. Clocks also can be used for other things, such as turning on decorative lights and fountains.

Electromechanical and Mechanical Timers

Time clocks are run by small electric motors and allow for many on/off settings during a 24-hour day. A pool time clock is different from other time clocks in that it has only one hand, which remains still while the clock face rotates. Each appliance requires its own clock. For example, if you want to run the pump during the day and activate the pool lights at night, two clocks are needed.

On and off trippers are used to set the clock. The words "on" and "off" are labeled on the trippers. Set them for the desired times, and the clock will control the flow of electricity to a specific piece of machinery. Screw terminals are located at the bottom of the clock so that it can be attached to the wires of the appliance (motor, light fixture, and the like). Electricity flows through the clock from a household circuit breaker.

A pool pager, above and right, tests your pool chemicals and signals you when maintenance is needed.

Twist Timers. These devices are similar to the timers found on kitchen ranges. They can be set for a specific period of time, usually up to 60 minutes, and let you know when the time has elapsed.

Twist timers are handy and safe because there is no way to forget to turn them off. This is important in a spa, where people often do not realize how much time has passed and would stay in the spa for too long if not for the timer. Twist timers are also good for controlling lighting that is not meant to be left on all night.

Electronic Timers. Unlike the mechanical devices described above, electronic controls have digital readouts and electronic circuits to keep the equipment running on time. These devices offer pinpoint accuracy, and they op-

Smart Tip

Be sure to keep all operating instructions for electronic timers. Many times, what appears to be a problem with the filtration or heating system is simply incorrect programming.—D.S.

A twist timer, on the deck of the indoor spa above, enables you to have your spa ready after a strenuous workout.

A television and speaker system, right and below, allows you to relax in your spa while watching your favorite television show.

erate on a very small amount of electricity. The voltage required by some devices is so small that they may be installed where they can get wet without causing a problem. Many spa packages feature electronic controls built into the shell of the unit.

Remote Controls

The same idea that lets you control your television, DVD, and sound system without leaving your chair is also used to control your pool and spa. Remote controls offer the convenience of heating up the spa or turning on the pool lights before you actually go outside.

Air Switches. These are the simplest forms of remote controls and consist of a hose filled with compressed air. Depress a button at one end, and you can turn a device on or off at the other end.

These switches are definitely at the low-tech end of the spectrum, but they are reliable. However, an air leak in the hose disables the switching ability. Hoses should be installed in conduit and buried to prevent leaks.

Wireless Controls. The twenty-first century version of air switches is the wireless control unit. Basically, these devices send a radio signal to a receiver. You push a button in your family room, and the receiver gets the signal out by the pool or spa and turns on the light or revs up the heater. Some systems are battery-operated, but others work on household current.

Many wireless controls can be activated through the telephone. Give the unit a call while driving home, and the spa will be ready and waiting for you by the time you get there.

Say goodbye to reaching for spa dials with a waterproof remote, left.

Make sure your diving board, below, is periodically checked for safety reasons.

A fiberglass slide, opposite, is easy to install and it's a fun accessory for kids.

DIVING BOARDS AND MORE

Diving boards are made out of wood for flexibility, covered with fiberglass to make them waterproof, and topped with a nonskid surface. They are available in spring-assisted and simple platform models. Most boards for home use are 6 to 12 feet long and 18 inches wide. To accommodate even the smallest diving board, a pool must be at least 8½ feet deep, 15 feet wide, and 28 feet long.

The base of a diving board is usually set in concrete. As diving boards age they can become dangerous and must be replaced. The signs of age include a warped surface, visible cracks, and a crackling sound when the board is used. If the fiberglass cover cracks or delaminates, it may cause the board's wooden interior to rot. A cracked board cannot be cosmetically repaired; there is a danger that it may snap. The only course of action in this case is to replace the board.

However, the sun can destroy the nonskid material on top of the board. Replacing this material is the only repair that can be made safely to a diving board. Buy a surfacing kit and follow manufacturer's instructions.

But before ordering a diving board for your pool, check with your insurance company (for coverage) and the building department in your town. Some municipal codes prohibit the installation of a diving board with a residential pool.

Slides

Slides are made of fiberglass and have metal stairs and frames. Straight slides are 8 to 13 feet long and use up significant space on the pool deck. Curved slides that take up less space are ideal for limited deck areas. As with a diving board, the higher the slide, the deeper the water must be in that part of the pool.

To attach a slide to the pool deck, the builder will either drill holes in the deck and set the legs of the slide in concrete or sink fasteners in the concrete and then attach the slide to the fasteners. In either case, it is a good idea to make sure the slide is securely attached to the deck before using it. A wobbly slide indicates a problem that must be corrected immediately.

Many people like to have water running down the slide to make the surface more slippery. Running a water line from the house for this purpose can be wasteful. Water ends up in the pool, but if the volume is too great it could increase the water level to a point where you will have to drain some of the water from the pool.

Attaching a line to the pool's circulation system is a better idea. However, you may have a problem with water evaporating from the surface of the slide. If you use this method to keep the slide wet, pay close attention to the water level of the pool.

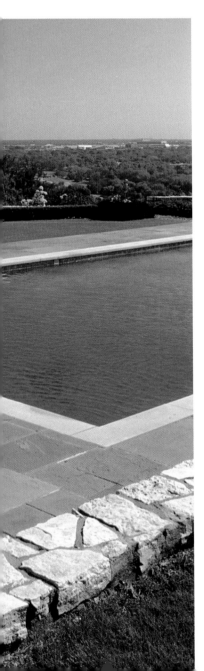

Pool safety depends on rails that are securely mounted into the pool deck, above.

Round-shaped rails in this lap pool, left, offer a different look than the conventional rail style.

Ladders and Rails

A good safety measure for pools that are more than 20 feet wide is to have a ladder on both sides of the deep end. Ladders must consist of at least two steps below the normal water level (approximately 24 inches) and handrails that are 17 to 24 inches apart to accommodate the average swimmer.

Rails are best located in the middle of the entry steps found at the shallow end. Your builder can also install horizontal rails along the sides of the pool just below the water line. These may come in handy for elderly swimmers or someone who has a disability and needs assistance while in the pool.

Ladders and rails are most often installed in mounting cups and then fastened with special hardware, usually a series of bolts and wedges. The hardware is covered over by escutcheon plates. Some builders prefer to remove a section of concrete and then sink the legs directly into fresh concrete.

AUTOMATIC POOL CLEANERS

There are three types of automatic cleaners: booster-pump systems, skimmer systems, and in-floor systems.

Booster-Pump Systems

Booster-pump systems take water that is already on its way back to the pool (after going through the filter and heater) and turbocharge, or further pressurize, it by running it through a separate pump or motor. This high-pressure stream of water passes through flexible hoses into a cleaner that roams the pool. There are two common types of booster-pump cleaning systems: vacuum head and sweep head.

Vacuum Head. The vacuum-head cleaner has a catch bag for collecting debris. Pressurized water from the booster pump enters through the stalk (a port on the top of the cleaner). Some of the water is blasted out of the tail, stirring up dirt on the pool bottom so that it can be filtered by the pool's circulation system. The rest of the water powers a turbine on a horizontal shaft that turns the wheels and moves the unit forward. Some water is diverted to a thrust jet, which can be adjusted up or down to keep the unit from moving nose-up. The head float keeps the unit in an upright position.

Sweep Head. The sweep-head cleaner floats on the water and has long, flexible, swirling arms that stir up debris found along the pool walls and bottom. The head floats on the water and travels around the pool by way of a bottom-mounted propeller that is fed by the booster pump. The main drain uses suction to pull the agitated debris into its basket, which is removed and emptied when full. The finer dirt is caught in the filter.

Skimmer Systems

Automatic pool cleaners that connect to the pool's skimmer use the suction from the skimmer to constantly vacuum the pool. A standard vacuum hose 1½ inches in diameter connects the skimmer suction opening and the vacuum head that patrols the pool bottom.

The only trick to keeping a skimmer-connected automatic pool cleaner functioning efficiently is to keep the pump strainer pot clean. As the vacuum patrols the pool, it collects leaves and other debris and sends it to the pump strainer pot. When the pot fills with waste, suction is dramatically reduced, causing the cleaner to become inefficient. To prevent this, clean out the strainer pot or

Smart Tip

Never operate a booster-pump system unless the circulation pump is working as well. Running it dry causes the pump to overheat and warp or burn out the seal.—D.S.

add a leaf-collecting canister to the vacuum hose. A simple in-line canister is easier to clean than the pump strainer pot.

In-Floor Systems

In-floor systems, used on concrete pools and installed at the time the pool is built, are plumbed to the pool's circulation system. As water returns to the pool from the heater, it is diverted to the cleaning heads in the bottom of the pool. The heads pop up and spray a jet of water that pushes dirt towards the main drain.

A sweep-head cleaner helps to keep dirt and debris off the wall and floor of this pool.

Automatic cleaners, such as this robot model, right, cut down on routine pool maintenance chores.

An aboveground pool cleaner, below, attaches to the system's pump and filter to provide the cleaning action.

OTHER FUN STUFF

If you are like most new pool or spa owners, the need for some products won't become apparent until you have used the pool or spa for a month or two. Most of these items will be games to make the experience more enjoyable, but other items will have more practical uses.

In some areas, the need for shade over or near the pool won't be evident until the hottest summer months. You can add a permanent gazebo or arbor or install temporary shade structures. The choice here is between poolside shade and structures that cover part of or the entire swimming area. Many of these newer tents are made of specially woven polyethylene rather than canvas because they can filter out the hot sun without trapping heat.

Other accessories include alarms that let you know when someone is in the pool and gauges that monitor the water level and signal you if the level drops below a

A water-level gauge, above, tells you when the water level gets low. Some add water automatically.

A towel tree, below, provides a way to air-dry towels while keeping them close by.

A basketball game, above, includes backboard, rim, support, and two balls designed for pool use.

An adjustable volleyball net, right, can span a pool that's up to 30 feet wide. This model includes water-filled bases with quick-drain plugs.

set point. These devices can help you keep the water above the skimmer level, preventing damage to the pool pump.

And what pool party would be complete without games? Pool and speciality stores carry all wet versions of the favorites: volleyball, basketball, golf, ring toss, and dozens of different types of squirt guns. When shopping, buy only products designed to stand up to chlorinated water, and stay away from anything with sharp edges. Toys and games make a session in the pool more fun, but be sure that young children are supervised while playing.

POOL LIGHTING

Lighting is essential if the pool or spa is to be used at night. There are three types of lighting for residential in-ground pools and spas: standard-line voltage—using 120- or 240-volt circuits like the ones used inside your house—low voltage, and fiber optics.

Standard Voltage

Pool lights that operate on standard voltage systems are mounted in a watertight niche that is built into the wall of the pool or in-ground spa during the construction phase (portable spas tend to have built-in lighting). The light fixture is made of stainless steel and shaped like a cone that's about 8 inches in diameter and 6 to 10 inches deep. A waterproof conduit travels away from the niche to the aboveground junction box.

When the light fixture is installed, the electrician will add extra cord that is curled inside the watertight niche. This extra cord is important because when it is time to change a bulb or replace the fixture, you must remove the fixture lens and allow the fixture to float out of the niche. The extra cord provides the slack for this type of maintenance.

Fixtures and Bulbs. Pool lights come in 120 or 240 volts; 120-volt lights are the most common for residential use. As with a household lamp, light fixtures are rated to accept various-size bulbs, generally from 200 to 500 watts. Spa lights are in the 100- to 200-watt range, and many spas use halogen light fixtures, which provide bright light but consume less electricity. A standard fixture lens is clear, but most manufacturers offer a variety of plastic color covers. If the fixture becomes rusted or otherwise damaged, it cannot be fixed. The entire fixture has to be replaced.

Caution: a light fixture is completely watertight and so the air inside of it becomes extremely hot. Without the cooling contact of water, the light will overheat. Never turn on a pool light unless there is water in the pool.

Pool lights, below, are important for night swimming because they let you gauge how deep the water is.

The pool, spa, and the surrounding areas, right, all benefit from a well-planned lighting design.

Low-Voltage and Fiber Optics

There are also some low-voltage systems, much like low-voltage landscape lighting. In these systems, a step-down transformer converts line voltage to 24 volts. Low-voltage systems are very energy efficient, but they do not produce the high light levels necessary for pools. However, spas often use low-voltage systems for mood lighting.

Fiber Optics. A fiber-optic cable carries light rather than electricity. In its basic form, a fiber-optic system captures light generated at one end of the cable, moves the light beams along the cable, and then terminates at a fixture, shining light into the pool. The light moves along the cable by continually bouncing off the reflective sides of the interior of the cable. Fiber-optic cables can also produce ribbons of light.

The big advantage of fiber-optic lighting is that the actual electricity used to generate the beams never gets near the water.

Fiber-optic lights, above, appear like shimmering stars reflected in this pool at night.

Canisters along the pool's edge, below, reinforce the geometrical lines of the home's modern architecture.

CHAPTER 5

Sparkling Water

A proper filtration system will remove relatively large particles of debris from a pool and spa, but it can't do anything about the bacteria and algae spores that will also find their way into the water. Rain, air-borne microorganisms, and even swimmers can compromise the quality of the water. As the owner of a pool or spa, you will have to do some things to keep the water crystal clear, clean, and pleasant, especially for when you and others want to swim or soak.

Water treatment sometimes makes people hesitant about owning a pool or spa. True, the science of water and its effective treatment can be intimidating if your high school chemistry class is a distant memory. Fortunately, most of the products you will use are adequately labeled and come with easy-to-follow directions. After a few months, you will know what it takes to keep your water pristine. You will also learn how environmental conditions can quickly change your pool's chemistry. A heavy rainstorm that adds untreated water to your pool, or a large pool party that puts a heavy demand on the cleaning system, can render the strictest water-treatment schedule useless, making it necessary to adapt to the new condition. You can always consult a local pool dealer, but it's also a good idea to understand what goes on in the water and how to treat it.

CLEAN WATER: THE BASICS

Some terrible things can happen to the water in your pool. It can become cloudy, turn a nasty color, leave stains on the surface of the pool, sting the eyes of swimmers, and even interfere with the workings of pumps and filters. The goal, of course, is to prevent any of that from happening. Pool water should be clean enough to see clearly a coin thrown into the deep end, and it should feel good on the skin. The only way to achieve those results is to kill off bacteria with a disinfectant, get rid of organic matter through oxidation—the breaking down of material at the molecular level—and keep the basic elements of the water in balance with one another. In fact, pool and spa water chemistry is really a balancing act. Even though it may not be apparent, a change in one component can affect the entire chemistry of the pool.

Most homeowners use either chlorine or bromine to purify the water in their pools or spas. Chlorine is the best-known sanitizer and for years was the only one available, but in recent years bromine has become increasingly popular. In some areas, bromine has overtaken chlorine as the product of choice.

Clear water, above, lets you see all of the details of this pool's handsome tile mosaic.

A sheeting waterfall, opposite, looks refreshing pouring into a pristine pool.

MAINTENANCE SCHEDULE AT A GLANCE

THERE IS MORE ON MAINTENANCE in Chapter 7, but because you are considering having a pool built, it is a good idea to know something about the maintenance routine.

Daily:
• Remove leaves or other debris from the surface of the pool. It is easier to take care of items on the surface than it is to deal with them once they sink to the bottom.
• Clean the skimmer and pump baskets.
• Test and adjust, if necessary, pH levels.
• Test and adjust, if necessary, the disinfectant levels.

Plants and trees can shed debris into the pool, but proper maintenance should keep the water clean.

Weekly:
• Vacuum the pool. You may need to vacuum more often after a heavy rain.
• Clean up any scum that accumulates at the waterline.
• Clean or backwash the filter.
• Shock the pool water by giving an extra large dose of chlorine.
• Hose down the pool deck.

Chlorine

Chlorine is popular because it is both an oxidizer and a sanitizer, and it is relatively inexpensive. You can buy chlorine in liquid, tablet, or granular form. (See "The Forms of Chlorine," right.) Chlorine is also available as a gas. (See "Saltwater Chlorination," page 102.)

When you add chlorine to the water, it goes to work immediately. To keep the pool clean, a certain amount of chlorine always has to remain in the water to constantly destroy subsequent bacteria and organic material. That means that at any given time there are two types of chlorine present in the pool. The type that is standing by to clean up the water is called free available chlorine (FAC). Then there is the chlorine that has already done its work and has combined with organic matter, called combined available chlorine (CAC), which is actually a compound made up of chlorine and nitrogen or ammonia. Together FAC and CAC comprise the total available chlorine in a pool or spa.

Think of it this way: FAC is good chlorine; CAC is bad chlorine because it no longer has the ability to sanitize the

Smart Tip

Give your pool service company a reasonable amount of time to solve a pool sanitation problem before switching. Changing companies frequently means using a different course of treatment, which may not be compatible with the original regimen. My advice: stick it out. If after a few treatments the problem persists, then look elsewhere for help.—D.S.

THE FORMS OF CHLORINE

CHLORINE is available in tablet, granular, and liquid form. Some types contain more chlorine than others. In addition, some products contain stabilizers, which keep them from losing strength in sunlight and heat. Generally, chlorine products that contain the most free chlorine and are the most stable cost the most. The following chlorine products are arranged from the least- to the most-expensive type.

Sodium Hypochlorite. This is the liquid form of chlorine and contains about 12 to 15 percent free chlorine. Don't confuse it with household bleach, which contains only about 5 percent chlorine. This product is very unstable.

Calcium Hypochlorite. Better known as Cal Hypo, this is available in granular and tablet form. It contains up to 65 percent free chlorine, and dissolves quickly in water. However, it is unstable and usually must be used with a stabilizer.

Dichlor. This is a tablet-form product that dissolves quickly in water. It is very stable and contains about 60 percent free chlorine.

Trichlor. This is a tablet-form product that dissolves slowly in water. It contains 90 percent free chlorine and is very stable.

water. The chlorine odor we associate with crowded public pools is actually CAC. When you smell chlorine it means that there is not enough good chlorine in the water. At high levels, CAC causes skin irritation and burning eyes. To bring the FAC chlorine levels to where they should be, you need to shock the water by adding about 5 to 10 times the normal application of chlorine to the pool.

Administering Chlorine. You have to mix liquid or granular chlorine with water before pouring it into the pool. Direct contact with the chlorine can bleach a vinyl liner. When handling chlorine, always use a clean container. Chlorine should not be combined with other chemicals. (See "Play It Safe with Chemicals," opposite.)

If you use a chlorine tablet, you can place it in a floating erosion feeder, in which the water slowly dissolves the tablet, or in a holder that you can install inside the skimmer.

Another option is to install a chemical feeder in the pool's circulation system. The feeders are placed downstream, or after the pump and filter. That means that every time the pump is turned on, the pool is getting a dose of chlorine, which is being distributed throughout the pool more evenly than is possible with hand or simple erosion

feeding. It also means that the chlorine is thoroughly diluted by the time it returns to the pump and filter, minimizing the possibility of damage caused by the chemical.

If you don't want to handle chlorine at all, you can install a chlorine generator. These devices pass an electric current through water that turns salt to chlorine. You refresh the supply of salt in the water by adding it a few times during the swimming season. In most cases you simply dump bags of water softener salt into the pool and move it around to dissolve it. Manufacturers offer charts giving the recommended salt levels for pools. (See "Saltwater Chlorination," page 102).

Maintaining Chlorine's Efficiency. Most manufacturers recommend keeping chlorine levels at about 1 to 3 parts per million (PPM) for pools and slightly higher levels for spas.

A sunny location, right, may keep the water warm, but ultraviolet rays can make chlorine ineffective.

A healthy spa, below, requires more chlorine than a pool does, because contaminants are more concentrated.

(See "Pool and Spa Needs," on page 108.) Spas require more disinfecting than pools. Think of a spa as a hard-used pool. Five people in a 700-gallon spa equal almost 200 people in a 25,000-gallon pool. Add to that the increased water temperature, which promotes algae and bacteria growth but dissipates chlorine, and you can see that spas often require more attention than pools.

Keep in mind that the ultraviolet rays of sunlight and heat can drain chlorine of its punch, making it unstable. Cyanuric acid added to the water helps stabilize the chlorine and increase its useful life. Most chemical manufacturers sell stabilized chlorine tablets, so there is no need for you to handle the acid separately. You should use a chemical feeder when using these types of products.

PLAY IT SAFE WITH CHEMICALS

YOU WOULD NOT BE ABLE TO SAFELY SWIM in a backyard pool without the use of chemicals or some other disinfecting agent. But don't kid yourself, pool chemicals can be dangerous if not handled properly. Cal Hypo, for example, may burst into flames if it comes in contact with some household chemicals. Here are guidelines for pool chemical use from the Association of Pool and Spa Professionals (APSP).

- **Keep all chemicals out of the reach of children.**
- **Keep records on all pool chemicals.** Some products have a shorter shelf life than others.
- **Store pool chemicals in a cool, dry place.** Keep them away from other household chemicals and equipment, such as items used for gardening and lawn care. This list includes things such as pesticides, solvents, paints, lubricants, and fertilizers.
- **Follow label directions to the letter.** Labels for pool disinfectants have been approved by the U.S. Environmental Protection Agency under the Federal Insecticide, Fungicide, and Rodenticide Act. If you can't read the label, don't use the product.
- **Apply chemicals directly to the pool water.** Follow directions for distribution through a suitable feeder or other means. This will also help distribute the disinfectants evenly throughout the pool.
- **Don't mix pool chemicals.** Use clean scoops for each chemical. When combining a chemical with water, pour it slowly and stir. Never pour water onto dry chemicals, as this may create splashing.
- **Dispose of wastes in a safe manner.** When dealing with a small amount of waste, it is usually safe to send it through the sewer system flushed with water. To be sure, contact the local health department for recommendations.
- **Take care of yourself.** Don't inhale chemical dust or fumes; wear eye protection when handling chemicals. Wash off any residues that get on your skin.

FACTORS THAT AFFECT DISINFECTANTS

MANY THINGS can affect the efficacy of a disinfectant. Here's a list of likely factors.

• **Bathing Load.** The more people who use the pool the more disinfectant you will need. You will notice an increase in demand after large pool parties.

• **Sunlight.** This weakens chlorine.

• **High Water Temperature.** Temperatures over 85 degrees shorten the life of many pool chemicals.

• **Wind and Rain.** These elements carry unwanted material into the pool.

• **pH Balance.** High pH levels slow down the disinfectant action of many chemicals.

• **Total Alkalinity.** Low TA makes it difficult to adjust pH.

Consistent tropical temperatures will require changing the pool chemicals more often.

Bromine

Like chlorine, bromine both disinfects and oxidizes unwanted material in the water. However, unlike chlorine, once bromine combines with organic matter (forming bromamines) it does not produce an offensive smell, nor does it burn the eyes and skin of swimmers. There is no need to shock a bromine pool because the compounds break down naturally. Bromine is also resistant to high water temperatures, making this chemical a good choice for spas and hot tubs or for heated pools.

On the downside, bromine is more expensive than chlo-rine. It also dissipates quickly in sunlight and cannot be stabilized the way that chlorine can, although you can add chlorine to help stabilize bromine. In fact, some bromine tablets can contain up to 30 percent chlorine. While a good choice for the confined area and high water temperatures of a spa, bromine is also an option for some large pools, particularly indoor pools shielded from the sun.

Monitor disinfectant levels, opposite, to keep water clean and balanced.

Alternatives to Traditional Chlorine

With the increased emphasis on environmental safety and the appropriate use of chemicals around the home, many people are seeking ways to reduce or eliminate the need for adding chlorine to their pool or spa.

Saltwater Chlorination. One alternative sanitizing method that has become extremely popular is called saltwater chlorination. In some parts of the country, saltwater chlorination has overtaken more traditional chlorine sys-

tems. But don't let the terminology confuse you. These systems DO contain chlorine. The difference lies in the way the chlorine is produced, how it is dispensed into the water, and how it feels on the skin.

Saltwater chlorination systems use a chlorine generator, an electrical device that converts salt into chlorine and continuously discharges it at low but effective levels into your pool. In simple terms, when water passes through the generator's cell, salt (sodium chloride) is transformed into hypochlorous acid (chlorine), which is the active sanitizer in all chlorine pool products. Chlorinators are in-line systems that are installed after the pool's filter.

There are two basic types of chlorine generators available for residential pools. The first, and most common type, calls for a small amount of salt—roughly the equivalent of one teaspoon per gallon—to be added to your pool water. The amount is so small that most people do not even notice it as they swim. The second method relies on a tank in the pool equipment area that contains a pre-measured amount of salt. Some professionals note, however, that these units can be messy and that it may be difficult to dispose of their byproducts.

There are a number of advantages to salt-water chlorination. Because the chlorine generator produces chlorine in the form of a pure gas that is pumped directly into the water, there is no need to buy, measure, store, or handle chlorine in liquid or tablet form. Because it is delivered in a constant stream, this low level of chlorine produces continuous protection against contaminants. As a result, there are fewer chloramines, the odor- and irritation-producing chemicals that are the byproducts of an out-of-balance pool. But according to its proponents, one of the greatest benefits of salt-water chlorination is the quality of the water. Swimming pools that utilize salt systems are said to have a smooth, silky feeling and are less likely to cause dryness and irritation to eyes and skin.

Alternative purification systems replace or reduce the need to handle chlorine and still have crystal-clear water, left.

Water purification systems work hand in hand with the pool and spa filtration systems to be effective, opposite. Both should be in top shape.

ALTERNATIVE PURIFICATION SYSTEMS AT A GLACE

HERE ARE SOME popular alternatives to traditional chlorine. Some products combine more than one type of system—for example, a metal purification system may include an ozonator.

• **Saltwater Chlorination.** Most popular system after traditional chlorine. In-line system that converts salt to chlorine gas, eliminates chlorine in liquid or tablet form. Components require replacement every 3 to 5 years.

• **Metal Purification.** In-line system that uses copper ions to sanitize water. Requires some type of oxidizer to break up organic compounds. Many systems include an oxidizer. Components require periodic replacement.

• **Ozone Systems.** In-line system that converts oxygen to ozone, a natural sanitizer. Reduces, but usually does not eliminate, chemical treatments.

• **UV Systems.** Ultraviolet purification is popular in drinking water systems. The UV light kills bacteria. Reduces the need for chlorine by up to 70 percent.

• **Biguanide.** Chemical alternative to chlorine. Not compatible with chlorine or bromine.

5

Sparkling Water

water, providing residual action for up to 10 days. And, the proponents say, these systems need to run between 10 and 12 hours a day to clean a pool. Some saltwater chlorination systems must run continuously to be effective.

NASA developed the basic technology for mineral ionization for the Apollo space missions. The companies that make these products have all added their own twists to the technology. So if you do decide on mineral purification, be sure that whoever will be maintaining your pool understands the system.

Ozone. You've heard of the ozone layer above the earth. But what you might not know is that the fresh, clean smell in the air after an electrical storm is actually ozone produced by the electrical currents in the storm. Ozone is a gas that oxidizes wastes. It is made up of three

Bright, sunny days, left, add to the maintenance requirements of pools and spas.

No matter which type of purification system you use, the water should be clear, below.

Many alternative systems, opposite, rely on more than one type of sanitation technology.

While you no longer need to add chlorine tablets, a saltwater pool is not maintenance-free. You still need to check salt levels and keep your water properly balanced; poor water chemistry can cause scale that may damage the chlorine generator cell. The cell will need to be replaced over time, although proper maintenance will help extend its life. In order to function properly, these systems require attention to make sure that they maintain a fairly constant salt level. Some manufacturers offer systems with automatic indoor controls.

You can expect to pay at least $1,000 for a chlorine generator, and up to several thousand dollars for a unit of the highest quality. The type of system you choose depends on a number of factors, including the size of your pool and the amount of time and effort you can devote to its care. Your pool professional can offer you the best guidance on your decision.

Metal Purification. These systems use the natural sanitizing power of copper, silver, and some synthetic compounds to clean water. This is an ionization process where a low-level electrical current generates ions from the metals. These ions kill algae and bacteria by changing their enzymes. They also tend to hang around in the

molecules of oxygen that are bound together. In that form it can kill harmful elements without producing any nasty by-products.

At poolside, a device called an ozonator draws air into a chamber and passes it in front of an ultraviolet light. The light changes the oxygen in the air into ozone. The gas then enters the pool water where it goes to work. As with chemical feeders, ozone gets into the pool water via the circulation system after the pump and filter. An ozonator will reduce the need for chemical treatments. However, you will still have to periodically shock the pool water with chemicals.

Biguanide Products. There is also a class of products that was created for pool and spa owners who want an alternative to chlorine. Biguanide (short for polyhexamethylene biguanide or PHMB) is the word most often used for these products, which are polymer solutions that disinfect pool water. Biguanide-based products are completely incompatible with chlorine or bromine.

Ultraviolet Systems. Finally, you can also use ultraviolet (UV) light to kill bacteria. In pools, a chamber located after the pump and filter zaps the water as it passes on its way back into the pool. The problem is there is no residual method for preventing bacteria. You will still need to use some chemical disinfectant in addition to the UV light.

KEEPING WATER CLEAN ON HOT, SUNNY DAYS

THE WEEKEND FORECAST calls for cloudless skies and temperatures in the high 80s. That's great if you're planning a backyard gathering, but not such terrific news for your pool. Strong heat and sunlight can deliver a knockout punch to pool water, severely reducing the effectiveness of certain sanitizers and spurring algae bloom. Add to that an increased bathing load—thanks to the nice weather—and your maintenance chores just increased. *Pool & Spa Living* **magazine offers these tips for keeping your pool crystal clear when temperatures rise.**

- Test your water regularly.
- Keep the water balanced and sanitized. Add sanitizer at night so that it will not be affected by the sun.
- Shock after a heavy bather load and before hot, humid weather.
- Consider the use of algicide as a preventative. (Ask your pool retailer for the best choice for this purpose and remember to brush.)
- Maintain the proper water level to keep filters and skimmers working.
- Run your filter 8 to 12 hours per day.

WATER BALANCE

In addition to sanitizing your pool and spa water, you must also keep it balanced, which is similar to keeping it tuned up. Pool and spa water that is balanced won't sting or burn the eyes and skin of swimmers and soakers. It also won't harm pool equipment or pool liners. In addition, balanced water helps sanitizers work more effectively. That's an important point because pool water that is out of balance will render sanitizers less effective, which means that you will need to add more chemicals. The elements you will have to take into account for maintaining balanced water are pH level, total alkalinity, calcium hardness, and total dissolved solids. It sounds more complicated than it is, but with proper testing and monitoring and by adding the right amendments when necessary, it isn't difficult to keep the water in balance.

pH Levels

The *pH scale* is a logarithmic measurement of the acidity or alkalinity of a solution, or the concentration of hydrogen or hydroxide ions, respectively. (The *p* is a symbol that indicates a logarithm of whatever follows it; in the case of pH, hydrogen ions.) If you have ever done any gardening, you know that experts recommend that you test the pH level of your soil before planting. The same type of measurements are available for the water in your pool. The results of these measurements are plotted on a scale that runs from 0 to 14. Water that measures in the center of the scale, around 7, is considered neutral. Anything below 7 is acidic—lemon juice or vinegar would be around 3. Anything above 7 is considered alkaline—the pulverized limestone you spread on your lawn to make the soil less acidic has a high pH, for example.

Water with levels slightly below 7 will sting the eyes of swimmers. Go lower on the scale, and the acid in the water will begin to eat away at tile grout, vinyl liners, plaster surfaces, and circulation equipment. At high pH levels the minerals in the water will begin to shake out of solution, meaning that they will form scale on the pool's surface and in pipes and other equipment. Obviously, you want to avoid both situations by keeping the water's pH around 7. Actually, it's best to keep the pH between 7.2 and 7.8. At that level, the water is safe for swimmers and it helps sanitizers work at peak efficiency.

Pool owners should test pH levels daily, or at least a few times per week. Adding soda ash to the water raises pH; adding an acid such as muriatic acid lowers it. As a pool owner you will be buying products that tell you what they are used for right on the label. Manufacturers package pH-adjusting products under names that basically say "this product raises pH;" or "this product lowers pH," such as pH Increaser or pH Reducer.

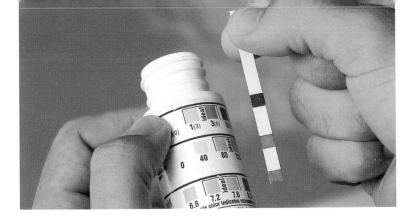

Kits often allow you to test pH levels, left, and chlorine.

The upkeep of a large pool and spa, below, requires daily maintenance.

Total Alkalinity

Total alkalinity (TA) is a measurement of the alkaline compounds in the water, and it has a direct bearing on pH levels. Think of a pH reading as a general statement that says one of three things: the water is fine; it is too acidic; or it is too alkaline. A TA measurement will tell you the exact amount of alkaline compounds that are in the water and whether to increase or lower them to get the water back into balance. If the water is too alkaline or isn't alkaline enough, it becomes difficult to adjust the pH so that it remains stable. Your measurements will vary widely from day to day, creating what pool experts call the pH bounce. For that reason, it is important to adjust TA before trying to correct pH levels.

Keep the TA between 80 and 125 parts per million (ppm) in gunite pools with unpainted finishes and 125 to 150 ppm for vinyl, fiberglass, and painted finishes. Maintaining these TA levels will stabilize pH. Sodium bicarbonate raises TA; muriatic acid lowers TA. Again, you will be buying products designed for TA adjustment.

Calcium Hardness

You are probably familiar with the terms *hard* and *soft* water. They refer to the amount of dissolved minerals in water, of which calcium is one. While you may want to get

POOL AND SPA NEEDS

YOU MAY FIND that some manufacturers of pool products suggest slightly different levels of the components listed below. But the ranges shown here are good targets. Note: ppm refers to *Parts Per Million*.

Chlorine	1 to 3 ppm
Bromine	2 to 4 ppm
Stabilizer	40 to 70 ppm
pH	7.2 to 7.8
Total Alkalinity	90 to 150 ppm
Calcium Hardness	150 to 300 ppm

rid of some of the calcium in the water that you use inside of your house, pools and spas actually benefit from what many people would consider hard water. If the water is too soft, it will become corrosive to pool surfaces and

Balanced pool water won't sting your eyes or harm the pool's equipment or liner.

equipment. If calcium is present in extremely high levels, it can form scale on pool or spa surfaces, especially at the waterline. Experts recommend keeping calcium hardness between 200 and 300 ppm, although it is not unusual to see recommendations from pool product manufacturers for higher levels. You can increase calcium hardness by adding calcium chloride or a proprietary product designed to increase calcium hardness. The only way to lower calcium hardness is to drain water from the pool and replace it with fresh water.

A pool that looks clear one day and then cloudy the next needs your attention.

Total Dissolved Solids

The pros call it *Total Dissolved Solids* (TDS), and it stands for just about everything you put into the water, including chemicals, minerals, suntan lotion, and the like. All of those solids are normally dissolved in the water. But water can hold only a limited amount of material. At a certain point, TDS build up to where they become apparent, usually in the form of cloudy or murky water. You may be doing everything right but the water still looks a bit off. Evaporation plays a large part in the build up of TDS. When TDS testing reveals levels above 2,500 ppm, even if the water still looks clear, it is time to drain and refill the pool. High levels of TDS make sanitation chemicals less effective.

OTHER THINGS IN THE WATER

Be prepared to deal with other items that end up in your pool or spa. Some relatively harmless objects, such as leaves and grass clippings, are more of a nuisance than anything else. However, ignore them and they may become a serious problem, so be sure to remove this natural debris daily. (See Chapter 7, " Pool Keeping—Routine Maintenance and Care," on page 136.)

Algae are another problem, especially in plaster pools. The word algae (plural for alga) refers to thousands of varieties of one-cell plants. The plaster surface in gunite pools gives these plants something to grab. The kinds of algae that turn up in pools are commonly known as green algae (chlorophyta), brown algae (phaeophyta), which may look yellow, and blue-green algae (cyanophyta), which often appears black.

Many pool experts say the best way to prevent algae formation is with proper sanitation and cleaning. That is true. But even the cleanest pool may sometimes develop an algae problem if conditions are right. Algae spores could be in the water you use to fill the pool, or they could be carried on the wind and fall into the water. Algae also need sunlight, warmth, and nutrients for food. Algae tend to be found on pool steps or in shallow water because these areas heat up faster than deeper water. They get their nutrients from the minerals in the water.

Remove algae with a combination of elbow grease and chemical treatment. Some types will brush away easily but others, such as black algae, are much more difficult to remove. There are a number of algaecides on the market to help you complete the job. (See "Resource Guide," page 224.)

Check the pool's steps for algae, which tend to grow in the warm, shallow water of this area.

Smart Tip

Occasionally, pool owners discover types of algae not usually found in their area. These new algae often hitch a ride on a bathing suit. Usually, the unsuspecting swimmer just returned from a trip. He or she went for a swim, then line-dried the bathing suit. The result: free air transportation for the algae. Avoid this problem by washing the suit in detergent and drying it in a dryer.—D.S.

CHAPTER 6

Creating Your Dream

A s with any large construction project, building an in-ground pool requires the skills of a variety of trades. The average homeowner should not tackle the project on his or her own. Aboveground pools and portable spas are another matter. Many of them can be installed by a handy do-it-your-selfer because they are relatively simple proj-ects that come with extensive installation instructions.

Even if a team of professionals will be doing all of the work, it is important that you know the construction process. The knowledge you pick up from this chapter will help you judge a quality job and will prepare you for what is about to happen to your yard. (See "Quality Checkpoints" throughout this chapter.) Construction is a series of messy and seemingly chaotic steps. The process may appear to-tally disorganized, especially at the beginning. But if you have done your homework and picked a good pool contractor, it will all work out in the end. The trick is to keep from pulling out your hair in the meantime.

At the start, things can be stressful as you watch your yard being torn up by heavy equipment. Construction begins with the contractor laying out the shape and size of the pool and the location of trenches for buried pip-ing in your yard. At this point he wants to tell the excavator—who is usually a

subcontractor—not only where to dig but what the dimensions are for the decking and final grading around the pool. The contractor will drive a series of wood stakes into the ground to indicate the size and shape of the pool. He may also draw an outline of the pool with lime or spray paint.

The excavator uses a backhoe to dig and trucks to cart away the soil. He needs about 8 to 10 feet of clearance to get the equipment into your yard. Be sure to discuss these requirements with the pool contractor before work

Pool contractors make measurement marks, top left, to determine the size and shape of the pool frame.

The excavation process, above, involves using heavy equipment to dig and to carry soil away from the site.

After installation, opposite, you can use extra soil to finish the area around the pool with colorful flowers or shrubs.

begins. You may find it necessary to remove fences, shrubs, or trees to allow access for the equipment. Excavation equipment is heavy and can easily chew up a lawn or crack a driveway. Speak with the contractor about making any necessary repairs before the job is finished. Check your contract to see whether it says anything about who is liable for this type of damage. For most pools, the machinery does the heavy lifting, while the final digging and shaping is done by hand.

The size of the hole will equal the size of your pool plus space to accommodate plumbing and setting material. The setting material depends on the type of pool. For vinyl-liner and fiberglass pools, the hole must be slightly larger than the pool itself because these types of pools require backfilling during construction. When backfilling,

QUALITY CHECKPOINTS

Make sure that
- **access requirements are discussed before work begins.**
- **the excavator does his best to avoid damaging your property.**
- **the contractor agrees to repair damage caused by heavy equipment.**
- **excavated material is removed from the yard.**

the contractor shovels sand or some other material against the outside walls of the pool.

You should decide what to do with the soil from the hole before digging begins. Some of it may be used for grading in the yard, or you may have some other use for it. If you are installing a vinyl-liner pool, some of the excavated soil may be used as backfill around the walls of the pool. But for many typical suburban yards, the pile of soil and rocks from the excavated site can be considerable, and it will have to be carted off your property by the excavating company.

Smart Tip

Many people want their pools built during the early spring so that they can enjoy the water most of the summer. Unfortunately, spring is the wet season in many parts of the country. Soft ground is not only harder to work with, it is also more susceptible to damage by heavy equipment. It is best to wait for the dry season before beginning construction.—D.S.

CONCRETE POOLS

For gunite (concrete) pools, it is not the hole that defines the shape of the pool but the gunite itself, even though it follows the general shape of the hole. Once the hole has been dug, the contractor will go over the excavation and hand-trim it. With the dirt and rocks now removed from the site, the contractor or the contractor's plumber lays the pipes for drains, skimmers, and returns that will be located inside the floor and walls of the pool. Some contractors also spread a layer of compacted gravel over the floor of the hole at this point.

CONCRETE POOL ANATOMY

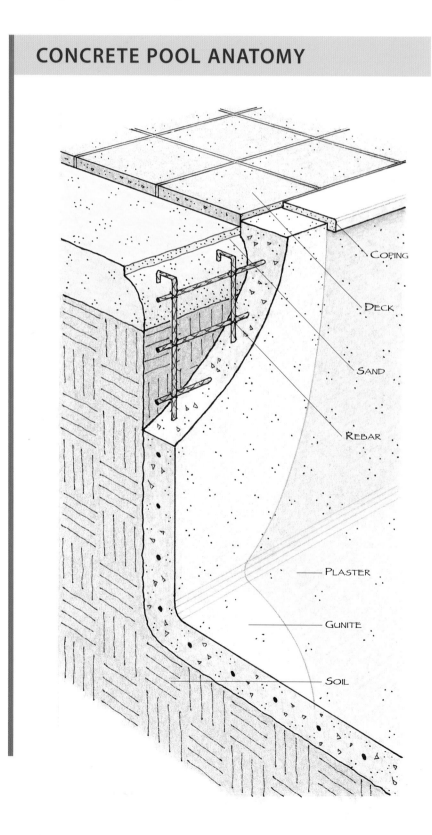

COPING

DECK

SAND

REBAR

PLASTER

GUNITE

SOIL

Molding the Shape and Reinforcing the Walls

The contractor lays steel rebar in a grid pattern on the floor of the pool and up the walls. He will do the same thing for an attached spa if it is part of the project. Where two pieces of rebar cross one another, he ties them together using wire. This creates a woven steel shell that is in the shape of the pool you ordered. The size and spacing of the rebar depend on the soil conditions and the desired thick-

The hole and the material used for the floor and walls or the shell create the shape of a pool.

Steel rebar, top left, is woven by the contractor and built in the hole. This creates a grid forming the shape of the pool that will soon be installed.

Gunite is sprayed, center, onto the grid to create the wall surface. Troweling the surface smooth must be done right away before the gunite cures.

Coping, which hangs over the pool's edge, left, is installed to create a smooth transition between your pool and the backyard.

Pool lighting, above, is installed by an electrician before the concrete is sprayed and cured.

ness of the gunite. Generally, heavier steel will be used at the top of the wall for the *bond beam*—the thick layer of concrete that supports the pool coping and deck.

Electrical Work. An electrician installs lighting fixtures and runs a heavy-gauge wire from the rebar to the common ground in your home's circuit box. This grounds the steel used in the construction of the pool. Should a short occur, the cable conducts the electricity to the ground and away from people in the pool. All metal that is part of the pool, including ladders and slides, must be grounded in this way. Filters, pumps, and heaters must also be grounded.

Spraying the Gunite

The gunite contractor covers the drains and other openings and then sprays the cementitious mixture around and behind the rebar. (See Chapter 2, "Diving In—Pool and Spa Styles," page 38 for more information on gunite and shotcrete.) He works on one section at a time, gradually building up the sides and floor of the pool to their desired thickness. The final thickness depends on the soil conditions as well as common practice in the area. Generally, gunite pools are 6 to 9 inches thick; bond beams are 12 to 18 inches thick.

Coping. With the gunite in place, the contractor installs the coping. Coping caps the top of the gunite wall, overhanging the pool slightly and serving as a transition between the pool and the deck or lawn that surrounds it.

Stonework and a sitting bench, opposite,
create an attractive finish around this pool.

Complement your concrete pool,
above, with handsome ceramic tile.

Coping is usually a masonry material. Precast concrete blocks, which are available in straight and curved shapes, are the most popular choice. Coping blocks slope so that water drains away from the pool. They have a slightly textured surface to provide sure footing for wet feet and a secure handhold for swimmers. If your plans call for a concrete or other masonry deck to abut the coping, the contractor installs an expansion joint between the two. This waterproof joint accommodates the different rates of expansion and contraction of the pool, coping, and deck materials, and helps prevent cracking.

QUALITY CHECKPOINTS FOR GUNITE POOLS

Make sure that
- the rebar forms a neat, consistent pattern.
- covers for drains and other openings are in place before gunite is installed.
- overspray is cleaned up.
- the gunite is of a consistent thickness throughout the pool.
- the plaster finish is smooth.

Curing and Finishing the Pool

After this flurry of activity, your yard may seem deserted for about a week as the gunite cures. Some contractors use this time to pour a concrete pad for the pool's pumps and filters.

When the gunite is cured enough to support a finish coat, the contractor applies a smooth plaster finish or an exposed aggregate finish to the pool. However, the top of the wall that will be above the water line normally receives a few rows of ceramic tile. The tile is attractive and much easier to keep clean than the standard plaster finish.

Adding the tile also means that all of the plaster in the pool will be below water—an important point because all of the plaster must be submerged to cure properly.

Filling the Pool

Filling the pool with water begins as soon as the plaster is applied and before it dries completely. Curing takes place under water. Allowing the plaster to dry and then filling would lead to cracking. At this point, there is a special startup procedure that you will have to perform in order to clean the pool of the plaster dust that accumulates in the water. (See Chapter 7, "Pool Keeping—Routine Maintenance and Care," page 136.)

Plaster Protection. Filling should be accomplished without damaging the plaster finish. If you're using hoses, wrap any metal fittings in clean rags or towels to prevent marring the plaster. Place the hose—gently—on the floor of the pool. Don't let water cascade down from the coping, as the force of the water could damage the plaster. The same holds for built-in fill lines. Don't let the water rush into the pool, even if it is being directed from a short distance above the pool.

This gunite lap pool was filled during the curing process, before the plaster was completely dry.

Smart Tip

Try to fill the pool as quickly as possible. Don't stop filling and then resume later. The water will leave a ring in the soft plaster where you stopped.—D.S.

VINYL POOLS

When we say vinyl pools, we are referring to the material from which the liner is made. These are pool packages that consist of a liner, support walls, and in some cases, the filtration equipment.

Constructing Walls and Support

The sidewalls on vinyl pools can be made of steel, aluminum, fiberglass, plastics, or pressure-treated wood. They are supported by a bracing system, which is usually proprietary to the manufacturer; either the manufacturer owns the company that makes the bracing system or has

VINYL POOL ANATOMY

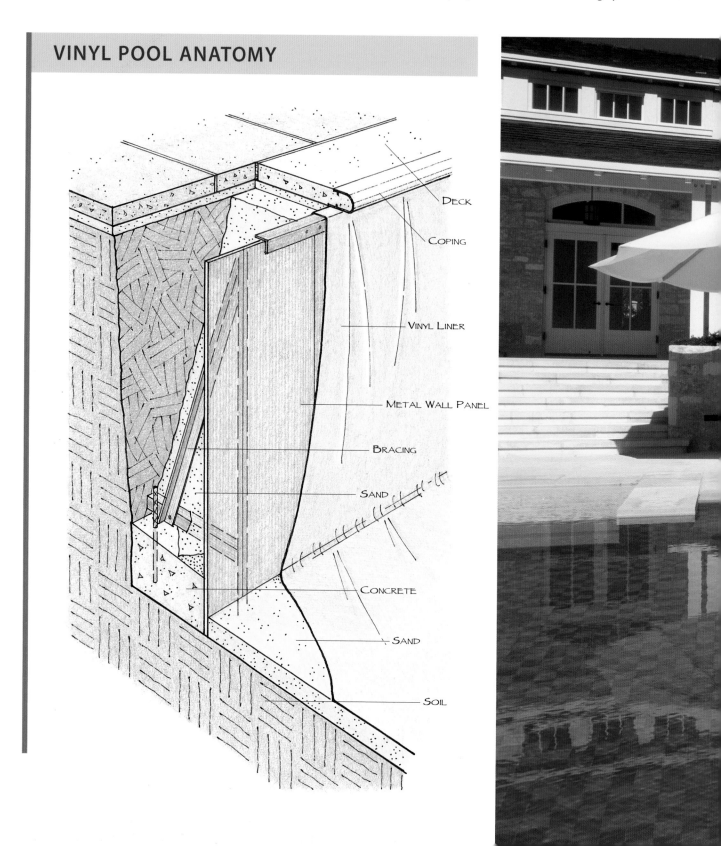

- DECK
- COPING
- VINYL LINER
- METAL WALL PANEL
- BRACING
- SAND
- CONCRETE
- SAND
- SOIL

an exclusive deal. Bracing systems differ from one another, but most form an X or an A to support the sides of the pool. The contractor sets up the supports and bolts the wall sections together. The most stable systems are those that anchor the supports in a continuous concrete pad.

The walls are either 48 or 52 inches high, so if you are installing a pool with a deep end, the area below the side-walls must be finished with either gunite or another cementitious material.

Vinyl pool installation is the same basic process for all manufacturers.

Installing the Liner

Vinyl liners hold the water and serve as the decorative surface. Even if your pool won't include a deep section, the contractor will cover the ground with sand or some other material to provide a smooth base for the liner. Plumbing lines are also installed at this time. Then the contractor installs the liner along the floor and sidewalls of the pool. Next, he attaches it to the top of the pool wall with coping and cuts out the openings for skimmers, drains, returns, and the like. Finally, he seals the openings against leakage.

QUALITY CHECKPOINTS FOR VINYL POOLS

Make sure that
- the pool base is prepared properly.
- sidewall sections are connected properly.
- concrete anchors the braces and sidewalls.
- the liner pattern looks straight and even.
- the liner is firmly attached to the pool's edge.

Finishing and Filling the Pool

With the walls in place, the contractor applies backfill in the area around the pool walls. Now all that is left to do is fill the pool and hook up the filtration equipment.

Sand is placed at the bottom of a vinyl pool, above, so that the liner will have a smooth base.

An expertly installed vinyl pool, below, is properly anchored, and the liner is secured to the walls.

FIBERGLASS POOLS

When you buy a fiberglass pool, the entire pool shell is delivered intact to your home. Obviously, the question of clearances for equipment is very important. You will need room to allow the flatbed truck carrying the pool to get close to the pool site and, in most cases, adequate space for a crane truck to move the pool from the flatbed to the hole.

But before the pool is lowered in place, all of the electrical work and plumbing must be completed. In addition, the contractor will have to prepare the excavated site.

FIBERGLASS POOL ANATOMY

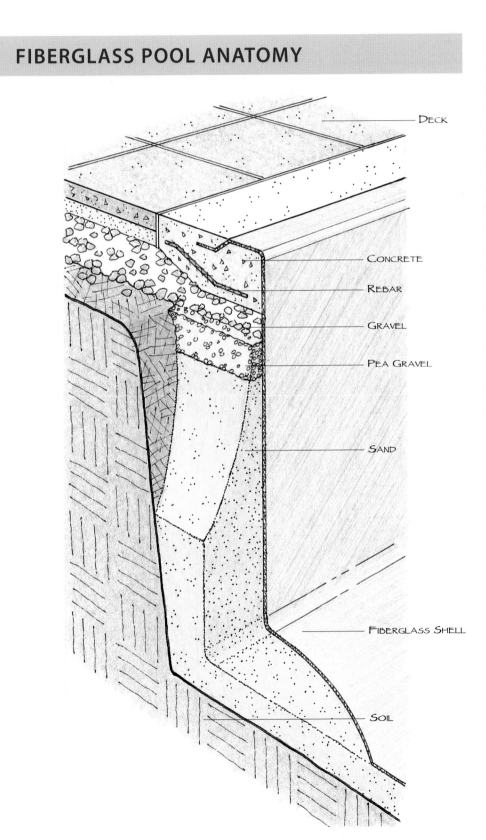

- DECK
- CONCRETE
- REBAR
- GRAVEL
- PEA GRAVEL
- SAND
- FIBERGLASS SHELL
- SOIL

Installing the Shell

Most manufacturers specify a 2-inch bed of sand as the base for the pool. As the crane lowers the pool shell into the hole, the contractor checks to make sure the pool is level. Sometimes the only way to correct an out-of-level pool is to remove the shell and regrade the sand. It isn't unusual to go through this exercise a number of times until the pool is perfectly level.

At this point, the contractor adds about 1 foot of water to the bottom of the pool to anchor the shell. Plumbing and electrical connections are made, and the pool is almost ready.

Filling the Pool

Because a fiberglass wall is relatively lightweight, the contractor must maintain equal pressure on both sides of the wall as the pool fills. This is an important installation point. If the contractor doesn't do this, the wall of the pool will bow out from the weight of the water. As the water level rises, the contractor keeps pace by backfilling the area around the outside wall.

Most fiberglass pool manufacturers specify sand rather than topsoil or fill as the backfilling material. Contractors "wash" the sand, which means they mix it with water so that it will flow easily into all of the voids around the pool.

Most fiberglass pools have a flange at the top of the walls. Digging out around the flange and pouring a concrete deck helps lock the pool into position.

Be sure to go through checkpoints to be certain that your fiberglass pool is properly installed.

QUALITY CHECKPOINTS FOR FIBERGLASS POOLS

Make sure that
- **the pool base is prepared properly.**
- **the pool shell is level in the hole.**
- **filling and backfilling procedures are strictly followed.**

ABOVEGROUND POOLS

The term "aboveground pool" can describe everything from inflatable kiddy pools to large permanent structures that hold thousands of gallons of water. Although this discussion concerns the latter, some of the inflatable pools offer the advantage of easy installation. Some are even designed to remain filled for an entire swimming season and then deflated and packed away during cold weather.

All of these pools come with instructions, but pool dealers typically install the largest, so-called "permanent" aboveground pools. Actually, an aboveground pool is only permanent in the sense that you may not have to take it down after the swimming season. However, you can disassemble an aboveground pool and take it with you if you move later.

Preparing the Pool Area

Although the soil conditions in your yard can add to the expense of installing an in-ground pool, just about any type of soil is fine for supporting an aboveground pool. The yard must be level, so some grading may be involved, but soil that is overly sandy or expansive won't affect the performance or add to the cost of the pool.

The contractor—or you—begins by removing the sod in the pool area. Many oval pools have side supports, which means that they need as much as three feet of space on each side to accommodate the supports. With the sod gone, the contractor goes over the area to locate the lowest point. He then continues to dig until the entire pool area is level with this point. Most pool manufacturers would say that if he had simply filled in the low spots, the fill would eventually settle under the weight of the pool and compromise it's structure. Not following the manufacturer's installation instructions may void the warranty.

After removing stones, roots, or anything else that could puncture the pool's liner, the contractor lays down a bed of sand.

The base of the frame, top, is set down on the level site where the pool will be installed.

The center is filled with sand, right, after the site is cleared of any objects that could ruin the liner.

QUALITY CHECKPOINTS FOR ABOVEGROUND POOLS

Make sure that
- the pool site is free of rocks, roots, or anything that could puncture the liner.
- the sidewalls are installed following the manufacturer's instructions.
- the liner is installed flat against the bottom and the walls.
- the liner is attached firmly to the pool's edge.

Assembling the Pool System

Aboveground pools differ from manufacturer to manufacturer, but most consist of a bottom rail to hold the wall, the wall panels, supports for the panels, the liner, and a coping system to hold the liner in place.

Contractors work from the ground up. In many cases, they install flat concrete patio blocks under the bottom rail to keep the structure level.

Systems vary, but for most pools the wall panels are fitted into the bottom rail and bolted together. Some wood-sided pools are made of individual tongue-and-groove lengths that fit together. A steel band encircles the pool, helping to hold the wood staves in place. To protect the liner from any sharp edges along the bottom rail, many companies specify a 6- to 8-inch-high sand cove along the bottom of the wall.

Installing the Liner

There are two types of liners: overlap and beaded. Overlap liners drape over the wall and are held in place by the coping. Beaded liners are fitted into a bead receiver at the top of the wall. In both cases, the installer makes sure that the liner lies flat against the floor and walls of the pool.

Aboveground pool siding supports, top, are placed in the ground during construction.

The pool liner, center, is held in place and flattened before its installation is finished.

The aboveground pool, left, is fully installed and ready for swimmers.

SPAS

In-ground spas are installed in much the same way as pools. In fact, many times an in-ground spa is built along with a pool. So it's not unusual for both the spa and pool to share the same lines for plumbing and electrical equipment. An excavator digs a suitable-size hole, and crews go to work building or installing the spa. For gunite spas, the contractor installs steel rebar and applies the gunite, finishing with a plaster coating that matches the main pool. For acrylic spas, the contractor either creates a sand base or builds a post-and-pier system to support the spa. Then the plumbing and electrical connections are made.

QUALITY
FOR PORTABL

Make sure that
- there is a suitable base.
- the dealer representative will level the p
  on the base.
- the internal equipment is not damaged during shipping.
- the finish is smooth and undamaged.

SPA ANATOMY

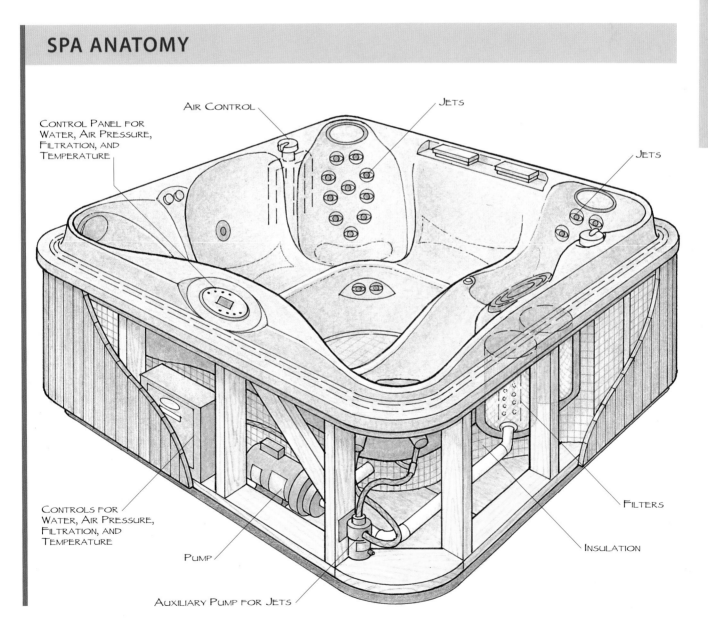

AIR CONTROL

JETS

CONTROL PANEL FOR WATER, AIR PRESSURE, FILTRATION, AND TEMPERATURE

JETS

CONTROLS FOR WATER, AIR PRESSURE, FILTRATION, AND TEMPERATURE

FILTERS

INSULATION

PUMP

AUXILIARY PUMP FOR JETS

Portable Spas

Portable spas—complete with filters, heaters, jets, and pumps—arrive at your home as a single package. While there usually isn't any excavation work involved, a fair amount of preparation is necessary. Aboveground spas require a level, firm base. Most manufacturers call for a 2- to 4-inch-thick concrete pad as a base for the large models. Paving stones or patio blocks suffice for small, lightweight spas. If you are planning a deck installation, check with a building contractor or structural engineer to make sure the deck can support the weight of the spa. A filled midsize spa could weigh over 2 tons, so if you are adding a spa to a deck, make sure it can handle the load.

Once the spa is in place and level, an electrician makes the necessary connections. Small spas require a 20-amp, 110-volt circuit. Many come with a GFCI-protected plug. Larger models run on a 50-amp, 220-volt circuit and must be hardwired to the main circuit panel or a subpanel.

Be sure to clear predelivery setup requirements, including necessary electrical work, with the dealer when you make your purchase. Some dealers simply sell, deliver, and set the spa on its foundation, which means that the homeowner is responsible for building the foundation and hiring an electrician for the wiring.

Heavy aboveground spas, above, need a firm bottom support such as concrete.

A portable spa, opposite, requires a stable site and proper support.

EQUIPMENT

Pumps, filters, heaters, and any other equipment you purchase is installed during the construction phase and then hooked up as a last step to the process. Deciding where to place the equipment is often a problem. It isn't attractive, and it can be noisy, so most people want it out of the way. But the farther away you place the equipment, the harder the pump must work to keep the system operating at peak efficiency. Straight runs between the pool and the equipment are best. Discuss this with your pool dealer because he includes the length of the piping runs and the number of turns in the run when sizing the

QUALITY CHECKPOINTS FOR EQUIPMENT

Make sure that
• the dealer provides a full set of instructions for properly operating and maintaining the equipment.
• the equipment is attached to a concrete pad.
• the electrical connections and grounding requirements meet code.

pump. You should be able to place the equipment as much as 40 to 50 feet away from the pool.

Installing Equipment

The contractor bolts the equipment to a concrete pad. This keeps everything level and reduces damage due to vibration. He should leave enough space between equipment to make service and maintenance easy. Ask to have gate valves installed on the lines going into and exiting the pump. That way the flow of water can be shut off if the pump requires servicing. The plumbing lines and electricity are then hooked up.

Plant lush trees around your pool, left, to hide pool equipment such as pumps, filters, and heaters.

A rocky landscape, opposite, also hides equipment while keeping it close to the pool.

CHAPTER 7

ROUTINE MAINTENANCE AND CARE

Pool Keeping

T he building crews are gone, the yard is clean, and the water level in the pool is rising steadily. Time to go for a swim, right? Not so fast. The pool isn't quite ready yet. Good everyday drinking water needs a few adjustments to become good swimming water. Basically, your pool will require a break-in period because tap water may contain a variety of minerals and algae, which can alter the color of the water. In addition, the pool itself will be dirty from the construction process. Once you fill it, all of that dirt and grime will be in the water.

During the break-in period, the filtration system will have to run continuously for 24 hours a day for a several days. While this is happening, keep an eye on the filter's pressure gauge. When it rises by about 10 pounds per square inch (psi) over its normal operating pressure, shut down the system and either backwash or clean the filter. (For more information, refer to "Maintaining the Filter," which begins on page 148.) Consult your pool dealer or builder about specific recommendations for breaking in your pool because the procedure will vary by pool material and geographic location. If you plan to hire a pool service to take care of regular maintenance, now is the time to do it. Experienced help will make the break-in process go smoothly, and pool professionals will be able to answer any of your questions.

the filter as necessary. Don't turn on the heater for up to three weeks and, of course, do not let anyone swim in the pool until the break-in period is over. After a few days, begin testing the water. Add chemicals to balance the pH, but do not add any sanitizer yet. Brush the sides of the pool, and vacuum it every day. Push all of the debris toward the main drain.

After about three or four days, add sanitizer. Test the water daily. Continue the procedure until the water is crystal clear and your testing has all of the components covered in Chapter 5, "Sparkling Water—Pool Chemistry Made Easy," on page 94, within acceptable limits.

ROUTINE POOL MAINTENANCE

Owning a pool requires attention on your part to keep the water clean and safe, of course, but you should also plan on performing some minor maintenance procedures to keep the equipment running at peak efficiency.

Every pool is different, and the requirements to keep the water clean differ for each one. The longer you own and use your pool, the more you will come to know what it needs. What follows is an outline for

Before opening a new gunite pool, left, allow the filtering system to run for almost a week.

Brush the sides of a pool, below, to remove grime that can eventually wind up in the filter.

Gunite pools with plaster finishes present a challenge. If you have a new gunite pool, it may take as much as five days or so to get the water just right for swimming. Remember that the filling process started while the plaster was still wet. If it didn't, the brittle plaster would crack when hit by the water. Filling the pool while the plaster is wet means that a lot of plaster dust is suspended in the water, and it is going to take a few days to get rid of it. As soon as a gunite pool is filled, you have to turn on the filtration equipment and run it for 24 hours a day—cleaning

Keeping the area around the pool immaculate and free of debris helps to maintain pristine water conditions and puts less stress on pumps and filters.

a maintenance schedule. It is a good place to start, but you may find the necessity to fine-tune it for your own pool. It is also important to realize that an established maintenance routine for a pool or spa only works when conditions are normal. A large pool party, using the spa more often than is usual, and even a heavy rain storm can change the dynamics of the water chemistry. When these conditions occur, you may need to perform some extra maintenance to make the water clean again.

Daily Maintenance

Plan on performing some maintenance activity just about every time you use the pool. If you don't use the pool every day, try to do some things every few days. For example, pick up a long-handled skimmer net and remove leaves or any other debris that ends up floating on the surface of the pool. Do this simple task, and you will save yourself or your pool service a great deal of work later. Anything that floats on the surface of the pool will sink eventually. Once debris makes it to the bottom of the pool, it is more difficult to remove.

While walking around the pool, scooping up leaves and grass clippings, check the pool's skimmer basket. If

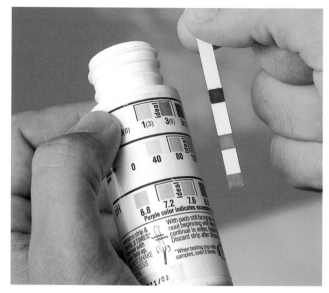

Use a hand skimmer, above, to remove leaves and other debris from the surface of the water.

Remove the skimmer basket, below, and clean out anything that has been trapped in it.

there is debris floating on the surface of the pool, there is also a good chance that some of that stuff has already been trapped in the skimmer basket. Clean the basket as necessary.

This is also a good time to check the water level in the pool. Evaporation accounts for much lost water over the course of a swimming season. That, combined with water loss from splashing and the normal motions of swimmers exiting the pool, draws down the water level. Make sure that the water level is adequate for the skimmers to operate properly. If the water level falls below the skimmer level, the pump could be damaged.

Water Testing

Test the water on a regular basis. There are a number of test kits available, but most homeowner kits fall into one of two categories: test-strip and reagent kits.

Test strips contain dyes that change color when you immerse them in water. The testing kit's directions will tell you how long to hold the strip under water—typically just a few seconds. Compare the wet strip to a color chart that is part of the kit. The color tells you what your pool needs with regard to sanitizer, pH, and alkalinity.

Reagent kits consist of liquids or tablets that you add to a sample of water from the pool. Again, the effect the reagent has on the sample in terms of color will give you a reading of the chemical balance of the water. There are two types of reagent kits: *colorimetric kits* and *titration kits.* Both are color-based tests. They differ from one another in

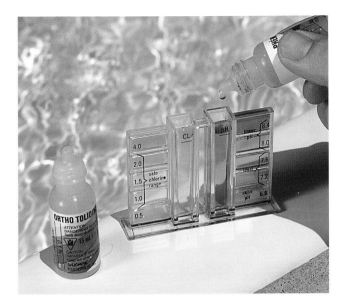

Test strips, opposite, are one way for homeowners to easily check the pool's water quality.

Reagent kits, above, like test strips, are a color-based test that come in liquid or tablet form.

The water level of a pool, like the lap pool below, must be maintained to keep the pump operating properly.

TIPS ON TESTING

- Always use fresh reagents or test strips.
- Rinse testing materials with the water that you are about to test. Never use soap or tap water to clean the equipment before testing as they can leave a residue that will interfere with the test.
- Run the circulation system for about 15 or 20 minutes before testing.
- Do not take samples from the area around the return outlets or from dead zones in the pool.
- Take samples from water that is at least 18 inches below the surface.
- Handle all chemicals and dyes carefully. Never pour them into the pool.
- Store testing materials in dry, dark places. Direct sunlight can harm the testing agents.

Smart Tip

If you do need to add chemicals, wait to see whether the chemicals have the desired effect. Wait about 15 minutes for liquid chlorine to circulate (with the pump running) and about 12 hours for the pH to adjust.—D.S.

that the titration test requires that you add an indicator reagent and then a follow-up reagent, which you usually add one drop at a time. The titration kit is the most accurate test kit.

Testing Alternative Systems. The alternative purification systems listed on pages 100 to 105 also require regular testing. The manufacturer of the system you select will indicate which types of tests to perform. Saltwater chlorination systems require testing for salt content.

Adding Chemicals

Most manufacturers print specific instructions for handling pool chemicals. In general, the goal is to get the chemicals circulating throughout the pool without getting any on yourself or areas around the pool. Again, refer to Chapter 5 for the types of chemicals you will be using.

Granular Products. Whether they are sanitizers, acids, or alkaline materials, granular products should be added directly to the pool and never put into the skimmer for circulation. Most granular products are concentrated, so avoid direct contact. The best way to do this is to mix the required amount with water in a clean bucket used only for that purpose. Slowly pour the mixture at various locations around the pool. Be sure to hold the bucket close to the water so that none splashes on you. Pour around the

You can hire a pool cleaning service to regularly attend to the upkeep of the water and the pool itself.

When adding granular chemicals, top, dissolve them or pour them directly into the pool.

While pouring liquid chemicals, above, make sure that the container is close to the water's surface.

The vacuum's collection bag, below, catches unwanted debris and dirt.

return inlets (making sure that the circulation system is running). It is also a good idea to add some of the solution to any dead zones, which are areas where the water circulation isn't as active as it is in other areas. Possible dead zones include areas around steps, corners, and alcoves.

You can pour granular sanitizers directly into the water. The problem is that they often take time to dissolve, so for a time they will be sitting on the bottom of the pool. This could lead to bleaching of some color surfaces.

Liquids. Pour liquid products directly into the pool. Again, hold the container as close as possible to the surface of the water to avoid splashing. Add sanitizers to a variety of spots around the pool, but avoid pouring directly into skimmers.

Tablets. Many homeowners find that 1- to 3-inch tablets are a convenient way to sanitize their pools. Placed in a floating dispenser, the tablets dissolve to add fresh chlorine to the water over a period of time. Be sure to check the manufacturer's instructions carefully. Some tablets are so concentrated that the larger versions are not recommended for smaller pools.

There is also a question of safety when using tablets placed in a floater. These are not toys, but they are sure to attract kids—especially a neighbor's child who may not realize that the floater contains chlorine. If small children will be using the pool, it is best to avoid using floaters containing chlorine.

If you do use them, try to keep the floater from being drawn to the skimmer. As with other chemicals, it is best not to add chlorine directly to the skimmer. Tie off a floater to keep it away from the skimmers.

Weekly Maintenance

If you attend to a maintenance routine that is daily or every few days, you will find that the larger tasks that should be performed weekly will go more quickly. If you contract with a pool-cleaning service, in addition to testing and correcting the water chemistry, the company should also perform other important tasks.

Vacuuming. There are two types of pool vacuums. One model attaches to the skimmer and works with the pool's circulation system to remove dirt from the bottom of the pool. Anything collected by this vacuum is trapped by the pool's filter. With the other type, water from a gar-

Smart Tip

The actual vacuuming, no matter which type of equipment you use, is fairly straightforward. Slowly work your way around the pool, down the walls, and along the floor. Move at a slow, steady pace. If you move too quickly, the current created by the vacuum head will stir up any dirt on the bottom.—D.S.

den hose forces the dirt into a collection bag. You remove the bag and the dirt with it. (For more information, see "Automatic Pool Cleaners," page 88, in Chapter 4, "Enhancing the Experience—Accessories and Fun Stuff.")

If you're vacuuming to the filter, be sure that all of the suction in the circulation system is concentrated at the skimmer you are using. If you recall the basic plumbing set up for a typical pool, you'll remember that the circulation system pulls water through the main floor drain and the skimmer on the side of the pool. Usually the suction created by the pump is about equal for both. But if you are vacuuming, divert all of the pump's pull to the skimmer. That may mean shutting down the main drain and opening up the skimmer valve completely.

Brushing. Use a special tile brush available at pool supply outlets to clean off the tile above the waterline. It may not be necessary to do this every week, but plan on doing it at least every two weeks (obviously, more often if necessary). Cleaning off the tile helps remove dirt and, more importantly, algae before it can take hold.

Plan on scrubbing the tiles using the tile brush and tile soap (don't use household detergent) about once a month during the swimming season. This is a good way to keep ahead of any algae buildup and it also helps remove scale. When you're scrubbing, reach down to clean just below the waterline because evaporation will force the waterline lower.

Use the above procedure on vinyl and fiberglass pools. Check with the manufacturers, but in most cases you can use the tile cleaner you buy at swimming pool supply houses. Never use abrasive cleaners, steel wool, or metal scrapers on these surfaces. They can tear vinyl liners and damage the gel-coat finish on fiberglass pools.

Keep pool tiles looking like new by routinely scrubbing them using a brush and tile cleanser.

In addition, check on the equipment at least once a week. See "Equipment Maintenance," on page 147.

Shocking, or Superchlorinating

As discussed in Chapter 5, it is necessary to shock the water by periodically adding massive amounts of chlorine. Shocking the water, or superchlorination, deals with the organic contaminants that build up in the pool over time. The contaminants combine with chlorine to form chloramines. It is the chloramines that produce the chlorine smell some people associate with pools. To get rid of the smell you must perform the seemingly contradictory task of adding a larger than normal dose of chlorine. You need to "shock" the water back to normal levels of good chlorine.

So how often is shocking necessary? Well, it depends on whom you ask. Most chemical manufacturers suggest a weekly shock treatment. That may be just the prescription for your pool, but in reality not all pools need a superchlorination treatment on a weekly basis. Pools need a shock treatment when there are large amounts of organic matter such as ammonia and nitrogen in the water. The more often a pool is used and the heavier the swimmer loads, the more often shock treatments are necessary.

Follow manufacturer's directions. Add chemicals to various spots around the pool. In most cases, you should keep swimmers out of the pool until the chlorine levels return to normal. Some products suggest adding shock treatments at night so that the pool water can stabilize overnight.

SPA MAINTENANCE

Spas require a maintenance routine that is similar to that of pools. But if the water in the spa or the spa shell itself is extremely dirty, it may make more sense to empty the spa and start over than to try to correct the problem. Shut down the system at the circuit breaker, and drain the spa. A simple submersible pump does a fine job of this.

Once the spa is empty, run fresh water through the circulation system to purge it of any dirt. Clean the filter (referring to "Maintaining the Filter," on page 148), and thoroughly wipe down the spa's cover. Use a cleaner on the shell that is recommended by the spa manufacturer. After you apply and wipe off the cleanser, rinse off the shell again. These cleaning products will undoubtedly be nonabrasive cleansers that won't foam up once the spa is filled again. However, it's still a good idea to rinse off as much of the residue as possible.

When adding chemicals to the spa, administer them a little at a time. Remember that you are dealing with only a fraction of the volume of water found in even a small pool. Go easy on the dosages. You can always test and add more chemicals later if needed.

Make it a practice to vacuum and clean the pool and spa at least on a weekly basis.

SOLVING POOL AND SPA WATER PROBLEMS

Problem	Possible Cause	Solutions
Cloudy water	Improperly working filter Algae growth Improper pH levels Dirt in the water Improper sanitation	Check and clean filters. Adjust pH levels. Shock the water using a sanitizer. Spas: drain, wipe down shell, and refill.
Chlorine odor	Excessively high chloramine level	Shock the water using a sanitizer.
Eye and/or skin irritation	Excessively high chloramine level Too much chlorine in the water (above 5 ppm)	Shock the water if tests reveal low levels of free available chlorine. If levels are high (above 5 ppm), allow the water to adjust naturally before using the pool or spa.
Corrosion on metal parts	Improper pH (acidic water)	For acidic water, add pH adjuster product.
Scale on walls and equipment	Improper pH (alkaline water) High calcium levels in the water	Add pH adjuster product. If adjusting the pH does not work and calcium levels are high, drain some water from the pool and all water from the spa, and refill.
Algae growth	Low sanitizer Improper pH	Shock the water using a sanitizer. Add commercial algaecide. Test and adjust pH.
Discolored water	Algae growth Excess metal in the water	Sanitize. Add algaecide. Add metal neutralizing product.

EQUIPMENT MAINTENANCE

The equipment that is part of the circulation system—pumps, filters, heaters, and chlorinators—also require regular maintenance during the swimming season. Each manufacturer will provide maintenance instructions, but there are a few easy things that you can do to keep the equipment running at peak efficiency.

Maintaining the Pump

Check and clean the strainer basket attached to the pump about once a week. This simple task will go a long way in keeping the entire circulation system in tip-top shape. To clean it, remove the top to get at the basket. While you have the top off, check the condition of the O-ring or gasket in the lid. If it is brittle or cracked, you won't be able to form the seal necessary to keep the pump operating.

If your pump is leaking, it is probably the seal that needs to be replaced. The pump consists of a motor that

Most pool circulation systems consist of a pump, heater, filter, and chlorinator.

PUMP TROUBLESHOOTING GUIDE

Problem	Cause/Solution
Pump leaks	**Broken seals.** *Replace the O-ring or gasket on the strainer pot, or replace the seal between the impeller and motor.*
Pump works, but the water flow is low	**Clogs may be preventing water flow.** *Check and clean the skimmers and strainer basket, or clear any obstructions in the piping system.* **Filter may be dirty.** *Clean as necessary.* **Pump improperly sized for the system.** *It may be necessary to install a larger pump.*
Pump is noisy	**There may be something stuck in the line.** *Check and clear.* **The bearings in the motor may be ready to fail.** *Call the pool service company.*
Motor is running, but the pump does not work	**Impeller may be jammed.** *Check and clear.*

The **strainer basket,** above, should be cleaned once a week to ensure proper system operation.

The **pressure gauge,** right, is located on your filter and informs you when your filter is clogged and needs cleaning.

turns a shaft, which in turn spins the impeller that creates the pumping action. At a certain point along the shaft is a seal that keeps the water flowing through the pump from coming in contact with the motor. This seal is made of rubber set in a ceramic disk. The rubber stops leaks, and the ceramic withstands the high temperatures created by the turning shaft. To get at the seal you have to take the pump apart. This is a job that is best left to a professional.

Smart Tip

Professional pool cleaners usually carry a waterproof marker to write the normal operating pressure right on the filter. If you are taking care of the maintenance yourself, you should do the same. Note the pressure on a new filter or just after you have cleaned the old one.—D.S.

Maintaining the Filter

No matter what type of filtration system you decide on—sand, cartridge, or diatomaceous earth—keeping the filter well maintained is an important element in making sure that you always have clean, healthy water. There are different maintenance procedures for each type of filter, and the manufacturer's literature will spell out recommended routines you should follow.

You will know that a filter needs to be cleaned when the pressure gauge on the filter rises about 10 psi above normal operating pressure—normal operating pressure will vary from circulation system to system. When the pressure increases by that amount, it means that dirt is clogging the filter medium.

On the other hand, if the pressure falls during normal operation, there is an obstruction in the system that is located somewhere before the filter.

Sand Filters. Sand filters are reliable and easy to maintain and can last for years. In these filters, pool water flows through a bed of pool-grade sand, which is sand with sharp edges to trap the dirt. When too much dirt is trapped in the sand bed, the filter needs to be cleaned by *backwashing*. This is the process of reversing the flow of water so that it moves up through the sand bed and out the waste port. Follow these steps to backwash the filter:

- **Shut down the pump.**
- **Turn the controls on the filter to backwash. Most manufacturers recommend backwashing for 2 or 3 minutes.**
- **Turn the controls to rinse, which purges dirt from the plumbing.**
- **Turn the controls back to normal filtration.**

TROUBLESHOOTING SAND FILTERS

Problem	Cause/*Solution*
Reduced flow rate through the filter	Filter media is clogged with dirt. *Backwash the filter.*
Low flow rate through the entire system	Obstruction in the system. *Clean the skimmer basket in the pool and the strainer basket in the pump.*
Filter does not clean the water	Routine maintenance has been neglected. *Backwash; if necessary, remove dirt from the top of the sand bed or replace the sand bed entirely.*
Filter needs to be backwashed often	Filter may be undersized for the pool or swimming load. *Replace the filter.* Careless gardening and fertilizing practices or use of the pool by pets. *Try changing the routine in such cases.*
Sand in the water	Backwash valve not reset properly. *Check and correct the valve.* Undersized or eroded sand in filter. *Have the pump checked by a professional.*

Many homeowners find that the simplicity and reliability of this procedure outweighs the drawbacks, namely the wasted water and the problem of dealing with the water once it leaves the filter.

As for the second drawback, you could hook up a hose to divert the water to a drain or sewer. If the chlorine level is below 3 parts per million (ppm) you could use the water that has been drained out of the pool to freshen your lawn or plants. Be aware, though, that high levels of chlorine will burn your lawn. Before using pool water on other plants, it is best to get the advice of a professional landscaper or county extension agent.

The sand bed should provide years of service. But there will come a time when the constant action of the water will round off the sharp edges of the sand, making the filter less effective. Individual grains could erode enough to pass through the filter and into the pool. Follow these steps to replace the sand bed:

- Shut down the system.
- Remove the top of the filter. If there is a mesh basket near the top of the filter, remove and clean it thoroughly using the hose.
- Scoop out the sand for disposal. When the filter casing is empty, add a few inches of clean water to the bottom of the filter. Add the manufacturer's recommended grade of sand.
- Reassemble the filter, and backwash it to remove any debris in the sand.

Diatomaceous Earth Filters. Most manufacturers call for backwashing diatomaceous earth (DE) filters on a regular basis, but there is some controversy on the effectiveness of backwashing these types of products. These filters consist of a grid that holds millions of diatoms, fossilized skeletons of plankton. These tiny particles catch and hold the dirt in the pool water. Backwashing will

TROUBLESHOOTING DE FILTERS

Problem	Cause / Solution
Reduced flow rate through the filter	Filter media is clogged with dirt. *Backwash the filter, or tear down the unit and clean it thoroughly.*
Low flow rate through the entire system	Obstruction in the system. *Clean the skimmer basket in the pool and the strainer basket in the pump.*
Filter does not clean the water	Routine maintenance has been neglected. *Clean the filter entirely, and add new DE through the skimmer.*
Filter needs to be backwashed often	Filter may be undersized for the pool or swimming load. *Replace the filter.* Careless gardening and fertilizing practices or use of the pool by pets. *Try changing the routine in such cases.*
DE in the water	Damaged filter grids or filter may have been reassembled incorrectly. *Check work, and replace parts as necessary.*

knock off some of the filtering media, which must then be replaced. The question is how much? Add too little DE, and the grid that holds it will quickly clog with dirt, forcing the pressure to build up again quickly. That means another round of backwashing. Add too much DE, and the material ends up jamming the system, which calls for another round of maintenance.

Many professionals end up opening up these filters and cleaning them on a regular basis. Follow these steps to thoroughly clean them out:

- Turn off the pump, and shut down the system and the circuit breaker.
- Remove the lid. Be careful not to damage the O-ring in the lid.
- Drain the tank of any standing water.
- Remove the nut that holds the retaining wheel in place. Remove the wheel.
- Remove the grids as per manufacturer's directions.
- Hose down the grids.
- Hose down the inside of the tank and the manifold.
- Reassemble the unit.

Note: You are not finished servicing a DE filter until you have new DE on the filter's grids. Running this type of filter without DE covering the grids will allow dirt to clog the unit, and you will need to break it down and start over.

Your owner's manual will tell you how much DE to add based on the size of the filter. Add DE through the pool's skimmer, allowing the circulation system to carry it to the filter's grids. Don't dump it into the skimmer all at once. It may clump, forming a clog somewhere in the system. Add a small amount, and mix it with the skimmer water. Add a little more, and wait a few minutes. Check the inlets for signs of DE flowing back into the pool. A small amount is normal. This was probably left in the system during the cleaning phase. But seeing large clouds of DE coming through the inlets is not normal. If you see them, it means that you missed something in the cleaning or reassembly. You will need to go back and check.

Problem	Cause / Solution
Reduced flow rate through the filter	Filter media is clogged with dirt. *Clea...*
Low flow rate through the entire system	Obstruction in system. *Clean the skimmer b... the pool and the strainer basket in pump.*
Filter does not clean the water	Routine maintenance has been neglected. *Soak the cartridge in a solution of water and trisodium phosphate.*
Filter needs to be cleaned often	Filter may be undersized. *Replace the filter.* Careless gardening and fertilizing practices or use of the pool by pets. *Try changing the routine in such cases.*
Calcium deposits	*Clean the filter with TSP; then soak it in 1 part muriatic acid to 5 parts water. Rinse*

Cartridge Filters. Filters that use cartridges are easy. Follow these steps to maintain good performance:

- Shut down the pump.
- Remove the top; most are held in place by a retainer band.
- Remove the cartridge, and hose it off.
- Check for torn or missing filtering fabric.
- Reassemble the filter.

At times dirt and oil will become embedded in the fabric and will not rinse off. Most manufacturers suggest soaking the cartridge in a special cleaning solution. Instead, you can soak it in 5 gallons of water and 1 cup of trisodium phosphate (TSP). After a few hours, or overnight if necessary, rinse the cartridge thoroughly with clean water.

At times calcium deposits can build up on the filter medium. After soaking the cartridge in TSP or detergent, clean the filter with muriatic acid. First test a small section of filter with the acid. If the surface foams, there are calcium deposits present. Remove them by soaking the cartridge in muriatic acid.

When gardening near the pool, don't let plant matter or fertilizer get into the water.

OPENING YOUR POOL FOR THE SEASON

If your pool will be closed down for the winter, you will need to take some steps to get it up and running again. The season opening involves raising the water level in the pool, hooking up the equipment, and cleaning the pool and the pool water.

The first step is to remove the cover without letting any water collected on it spill into the pool. If it does end up in the pool, and some probably will, you will need to add more chemicals and run the filter longer to get the pool into swimming shape. Begin by clearing debris from the cover. Then hook up a pump to get standing water off of the cover.

While the pump is working, slip a garden hose under the

Before it freezes, lower the water level but do not completely drain a spa, above, or a pool.

A year-round pool, opposite, requires just a few hours of weekly maintenance. However, cover the pool when it's not in use.

cover and begin to fill the pool. The water level rising under the cover will actually help clear the cover of standing water. Once you get the cover off, wash it down with soap and water and let it dry before storing it for the season.

Reinstall any equipment you moved inside, and give it a maintenance check. Look for O-rings and seals that are cracked and brittle, and replace them if necessary.

Run the filter system for a day; then test the water. You can also take a sample to a pool-supply retailer who will run a thorough analysis for you. Add chemicals as needed.

CLOSING YOUR POOL FOR THE SEASON

When it comes time to close your pool for the cold weather, you will want to clean it as much as possible so that the spring opening will go that much easier. The entire process can be broken down into three parts: cleaning the drain; sanitizing the pool; and installing the cover.

To clean the drain, first lower the water level in the pool to about 18 to 20 inches below the skimmer. Don't drain the pool completely. Besides needing to refill it in the spring and starting over with your chemical treatment, you're making an empty pool vulnerable to pressures from the sides and below. Freezing ground causes the earth to expand and heave, which could crack a gunite pool or severely damage a vinyl liner or fiberglass shell.

Next, sanitize the pool. Adjust the water chemistry, and shock the water. It is also a good idea to give the pool a final vacuuming and brushing.

You should also drain all of the water out of the piping system and any standing water that is in the pumps and filters. Check the owner's manual on how to drain the equipment. Usually there are plugs located on the units. You can also add an antifreeze solution designed for pools, which can be found at any pool supply company. Don't add automotive antifreeze.

Finally, install a tight-fitting cover over the pool. A good cover will keep out wind-blown debris through autumn, winter, and spring, so your pool water will stay cleaner and your life will be much easier at the start of the next swimming season.

Smart Tip

Some pool manufacturers suggest disconnecting the pump and storing it indoors for the winter if the pool does not get year-round use.—D.S.

POOL REPAIRS

New pool owners often mistake evaporation for a leaking pool. They see the water level drop quickly and figure there must be a leak. A dropping water level could actually be caused by evaporation, and there is a simple test you can perform to find out. Assuming the visible plumbing isn't leaking and there are no small streams flowing out of the equipment pack, conduct the evaporation or bucket test. Fill a bucket about halfway with water, and mark the waterline on the side of the container. Set the bucket next to the pool or even in the pool on a step or in the shallow end if the bucket is big enough. Mark the waterline on the side of the pool. Turn off the circulation system, and keep swimmers out of the water for a couple of days.

Compare the water levels against the marks you made. If the difference between the new waterline and the marks are about the same on the bucket and the side of the pool, evaporation is causing the water loss. If the level in the pool dropped by a larger margin, there is a leak somewhere in the system.

As with any type of construction, most leaks occur where two different materials join one another. A pool service technician will begin looking for the leak along the tile border, where the ladder is bolted to the side of the pool, and around the drain, inlets, and lights.

Pool dealers stock a variety of repair materials, including patching plasters and vinyl, fiberglass, and acrylic repair kits. If you are attempting repairs on your own, be sure to check with the manufacturer of vinyl or fiberglass pools to make sure that the products you choose will work on your pool.

Most repairs require draining the pool to the leak. There is a plaster patching method that lets you work underwater, but it takes some practice and should be left to someone with experience. Plan on draining vinyl and fiberglass pools and acrylic spas to patch leaks. These repairs are easier to make and usually involve drying the area, cleaning it, roughing up the surface, applying some type of bonding agent, and then applying the patch.

Indoor Pools and Spas

Because debris is kept to a minimum, indoor pools and spas tend to be easier to maintain than their outdoor counterparts. Check water balance and sanitation levels regularly, and inspect the equipment as needed. Also plan on installing a ventilation system with a dehumidifier.

One area that is often a concern is the accumulation of total dissolved solids (TDS). As emptying and refilling the pool or spa is the only way to correct this problem, many homeowners avoid this step in an indoor installation. If you are planning an indoor pool or spa, be sure to include a drain line that will allow you to empty the pool as needed.

An enclosed room with a pool or spa requires a ventilation system and a dehumidifier to keep the environment pleasant and healthy.

CHAPTER 8

LANDSCAPING AND WATER FEATURES

Around the Pool

Putting in a new pool or spa rarely means that once it's in the yard the job is done. Instead, it is just the beginning of a multifaceted endeavor. At the very least you'll need to add decking to surround it, a fence for safety, and perhaps a place for storing the pool-care equipment. But to fully enjoy your investment, you'll want to add other elements to complete the setting. Very often this means landscaping your yard to include things such as a larger patio or wooden deck for relaxing and entertaining, walkways for getting to and from the pool, plantings for privacy, and gardens for decoration. It may even be the addition of a water feature, such as a pond, waterfall, or fountain, that can complement the pool and the surrounding landscape.

Landscape design, however, is a skill that takes years of study and practice to master. Even home gardeners who can grow just about anything in their yards have trouble combining plantings with the necessary "hardscapes"—the decks, patios, and walkways—required when you add a pool or spa. Remember that a swimming pool or spa need not be a jarring element in your landscape. When skillfully designed, it can be an integral and attractive part of the overall design of an outdoor living environment. This chapter offers information, advice, ideas, and guidelines to achieving the most enjoyable and relaxing outdoor setting for your pool or spa.

SUCCESSFUL LANDSCAPE DESIGN

Develop a concept. Begin by identifying your style—your dream landscape—and list every feature, no matter how frivolous it may seem to be. From there, you can start to make it a reality. Be guided by the basic elements of any good design: proportion, light, color, mass, and texture are key to a successful landscape design. Keep asking yourself, "What makes sense for my property?" Establish a budget. This will determine whether you need to scale back and plan to do some of the work yourself. Start planning. Take photographs; make notes; and draw sketches to commit your ideas to paper.

Professional Help

Some people have a natural design sense, know exactly what they need, can visualize how all of the elements will fit together, and then also have the expertise to do the actual work themselves. But for those who need assistance with one or all of these things, hiring professional help is usually the best solution.

There are several professional options. For the initial layout and design of the yard, you have a choice between a landscape architect or a landscape designer. For the actual work, there are landscape contractors.

Landscape Architects. To be certified, a landscape architect must have graduated from a course in landscape architecture that includes education in engineering, horticulture, and architectural design. Many states require that this coursework be validated by passing the Landscape Architect Registration Examination (LARE), which tests the candidate's knowledge of grading and drainage, landscape construction, landscape design and history, and professional ethics. Because of their extensive formal training, landscape architects are more expensive to hire than landscape designers.

Landscape Designers. A landscape designer is knowledgeable about design principles, plants, and plant materials, especially those that are frequently used in his or her region. However, landscape designers are not required to have any formal training. Landscape designers are often employed by large nurseries that provide free design serv-

Landscaping around a pool may include recommendations for providing privacy, above left.

Hardscaping can include fences and trellises, left, that complement the pool's shape.

ices for those who purchase the plants from them.

Landscape Contractors. A third professional category, landscape contractors are individuals trained to do such work as laying patios and paths, building decks and structures, and installing plants and irrigation systems. Landscape contractors also carry out the construction plans of landscape architects.

If you have a complicated project such as one that requires grading for terraces or includes sophisticated drainage or hardscaping, you would be wise to hire a landscape architect along with a contractor. On the other hand, for a simpler project, and for much less money, a creative landscape designer can usually provide a satisfactory plan for beds and borders with a pleasing assortment of plants and shrubs.

If you decide to use both a landscape architect and a contractor, remember that you don't need to use all of their services. Most landscape architects are willing to draw up plans and then allow you to implement them at your leisure. You may need to call in a professional to build a terrace of retaining walls, but you may want to lay the paths and install the plants yourself. You are in charge,

and you can negotiate whatever arrangement best suits your needs and budget.

Creating the Plan

The first step is to develop a master plan of the area, such as the one that was drawn up when you were deciding on the location and installation of the pool or spa. This plan included existing conditions so that you could properly place your pool or spa. Now is the time to add your ideas for any new landscaping and hardscaping. Because your new pool and spa will definitely be the focal point of the yard, it makes the most sense to start designing at the pool or spa and work out from there. You'll have to make choices—from the size, shape, color, and texture of surfaces, to the types of trees, shrubs, and flower beds, and then where to place each for the best effect. Some elements, such as fencing for safety, will be required by building codes. Others, such as a water feature, sprinkler system, and lighting, that could be a future project should also be considered. Your finished plan should include all of them—new bushes, fences, patio, paths, flower beds, and so on that you want to add to complete your design.

CREATE THE MASTER PLAN

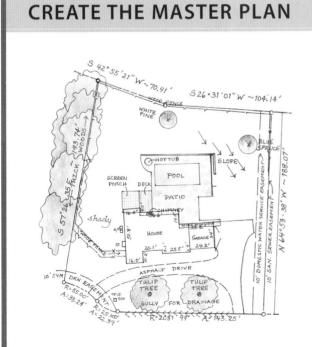

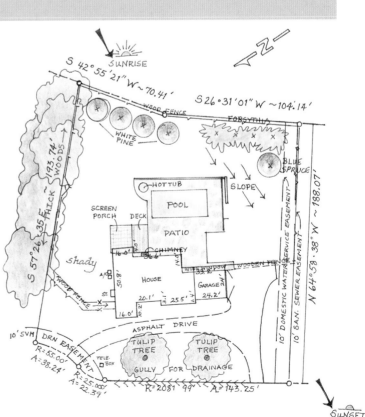

Create a base map of the existing property. A second drawing shows the addition of a fence, additional plantings, and where the sun rises and sets.

THE POOL DECKING

The paved area around a pool is often referred to as the decking. It is there for safety but it is equally important as a design feature of the entire area. It acts not only as a transition from pool to yard, but as a place where wet feet can dry off or as a location for poolside dining and entertaining. Although the minimum width for decking around a pool is 3 feet, you will need a much wider area to provide space for lounges for sunbathing and tables and chairs for dining and entertaining. Look for a balance between enough paving for adequate living space but not so much that it becomes a vast wasteland.

Concrete

The most common poolside decking is concrete because it is both economical and versatile. But if you would prefer a rough-textured finish, leave the aggregate exposed. In addition to being an attractive texture, an exposed-aggregate surface is less slippery than smooth concrete. Because people spend a lot of time barefoot near the pool, you'll want a fine, even-textured aggregate such as pea gravel that doesn't have a lot of sharp edges.

Another option is to tint the concrete. Choose a color that will blend with other elements in your landscape as well as give the deck surface a warmer feel. Tinted concrete also creates less glare—an important consideration where the summer sun is intense. Concrete can become burning hot when it is exposed to hours of direct sun. A more-expensive option is to have a special cooling surface troweled onto the concrete when your pool decking is installed.

Other Surface Materials

Other possibilities for pool decking include wood, paving tiles, blocks, brick, flagstones, and granite. Your choice should be guided by budget, as well as how the material will blend with your overall landscape design. Brick and flagstone laid in symmetrical patterns tend to look formal, while flagstone laid in a crazy-quilt pattern and wood decking are more casual. Flagstone and wood when wet, however, can be slippery, something you may not want to encourage around the pool or spa.

Brick is a handsome decking material that easily makes the transition from pool to home.

FENCES

Fences can define spaces, serve as property boundaries, provide privacy, or block a prevailing wind around the pool area. They may be purely ornamental, as well. But fences are also safety devices. In fact, most communities have regulations about fencing around pools to protect small children. See Chapter 9, "Worry-Free Fun—Using Your Pool and Spa Safely," pages 202–215, for more information.

Design Options

To be a successful part of a landscape, a fence should be planned to complement the architecture of your house, possibly even echoing a distinctive design feature. Also bear in mind the character of your neighborhood and region. Your fence may be beautiful in and of itself but look out of place in the neighborhood where you live. In addition, a fence should be harmonious with its surroundings in terms of height, color, and material.

Traditional options include wrought iron, wooden pickets (or palings), stockade, split-rail, double- and triple-bar ranch fences, and even chain-link fences. Within those basic styles are infinite variations.

A stepped-down privacy fence, above, was built to match the decking and spa surround.

Some of the soil that was excavated for the pool and spa was used for a berm, or raised planting area, below.

Latticework. A lattice screen or trellis is a way to achieve privacy or to partition off a space. The lath slats of lattice interrupt the view without totally obscuring it, creating the effect of a translucent curtain.

A wall of lattice fencing above, allows air to enter while creating privacy.

If a fence isn't needed, opposite, consider a vertical structure such as this pergola.

Erecting Fences

Erecting a fence is the quickest and generally easiest way to define the boundary of your property. It should have a logical starting and ending point. Like a chain, a fence is only as strong as its weakest component. If you are building a fence, be sure to choose strong posts and sink them properly into the ground. If you're building a wooden fence, you will save money if you design the fence so that you can use standard lengths of lumber. Otherwise you'll waste too much time measuring and cutting, and you'll end up with a lot of wasted wood.

Before you begin a do-it-yourself fencing project, check with local authorities for relevant codes and ordinances. Height and placement regulations (especially required setbacks from property lines) vary from community to community, and some residential neighborhoods have their own covenants.

GATE ANATOMY

Position a gate between its postholes, and line up elements of the gate and fence. Use spacers and shims to adjust it in the opening between posts, and clamp it as needed so that the gate won't move as you drill and attach hardware.

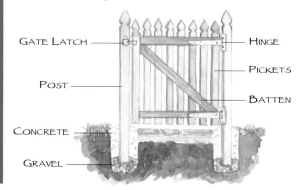

GATE LATCH — — HINGE

— PICKETS

POST — — BATTEN

CONCRETE —

GRAVEL —

PATIOS AND DECKS

In addition to the decking that surrounds the pool, an expanded patio or deck will increase the overall size of the recreation and entertainment area. The design possibilities for decks and patios are almost limitless. Squares and rectangles are traditional; they are the easiest to construct because the lines are parallel and straight. Decks are ideal for sloping lots because they reclaim space that otherwise might go unused. In cases where the main floor of the house is several feet or more above ground level, a deck gives access to the outside.

Another consideration is the location of the deck or patio. If you plan to furnish it with a table and chairs for outdoor dining, then choose a spot that's as close as possible to the kitchen but also convenient to the pool. No matter how inviting the finished spot is, if you have to carry all of your dining paraphernalia a long way, you will not want to bother.

Also think about the time of day that you will most likely use your outdoor space. For morning meals, an eastern-facing deck or patio will catch the early sun. In the summer, a shady spot protected from the midday sun would be pleasant for lunch. A deck or patio facing west will stay warm longer in the evenings, but may be too hot on summer days. If you have the space and budget, consider the possibility of more than one deck or patio to catch the light at different times of day. On a small property, a seating area at the far end of the lot draws the eye away from the house and encourages maximum use of the land.

Patio Design

If the patio is connected to a traditionally designed house, a classic shape may be most suitable because it echoes the symmetrical lines of the house. On the other hand, if you have a modern house full of unexpected angles and lines, you may want to try to re-create the asymmetric features of the house. Consider ovals, circles, or other geometric shapes for patios placed away from the house. To make it a delightful focal point and a desirable destination, furnish this distant patio attractively and comfortably.

A covered patio is the perfect spot for outdoor entertaining.

Plant around the patio to set off the space. Add containers full of plants to soften the paved area. If the patio is in a hot sunny spot, you may want to cover it with a lath roof or perhaps install a retractable awning.

Paving Materials. The materials you choose for paving a patio will depend on your budget and the style of your house and garden. The choice of materials available for patio paving is constantly expanding. Brick and flagstone are traditional, but you can also use interlocking concrete pavers cut to different patterns, poured concrete, exposed-aggregate concrete, and pebbles and river stones set in concrete. A wide array of tiles and paving slabs with premolded patterns such as cobbles, brick, or crazy paving is available. You might even want to border a concrete patio with brick and create a cobblestone design in the center.

The prices of paving materials will vary from region to region; importing stones and pavers can drive up the cost of your patio. Research all of the options. Visualize the color and texture of the paving material and how it will blend with the house and garden. Then choose the one that best meets your design needs and budget.

Deck Design

The basic elements of a deck are posts set into footings or piers, support beams and joists, the deck surface, and railings if so desired. Instead of running the surface boards in parallel lines, experiment on paper with different patterns

A multilevel deck features a spa area that includes a trellis and built-in benches.

for a more interesting surface design. You also may want to include stairs leading from a raised deck to another level or to the ground. Even a deck near ground level may benefit from a step or two to ease the transition from the platform to the ground. The railings can be horizontal or vertical. They can be spaced evenly or in an attractive pattern. You may want to insert a design into the railings such as a sailboat motif, a rising sun, or a pinwheel pattern. For a traditional look resembling an old-fashioned porch, insert milled balusters. For more privacy, build a solid enclosure. You could create a diamond, lattice design, or angle vertical slats for an interesting visual effect.

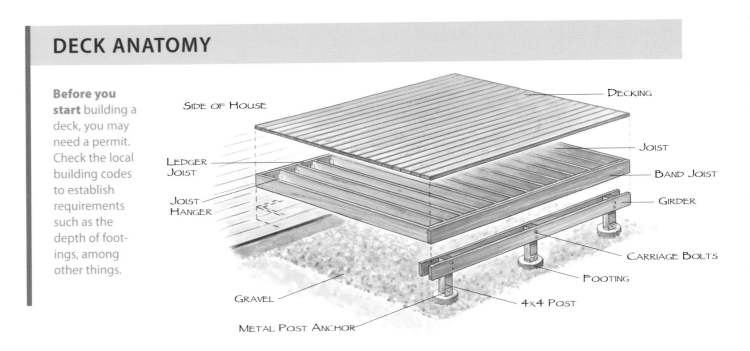

DECK ANATOMY

Before you start building a deck, you may need a permit. Check the local building codes to establish requirements such as the depth of footings, among other things.

SIDE OF HOUSE

DECKING

LEDGER JOIST

JOIST HANGER

JOIST

BAND JOIST

GIRDER

CARRIAGE BOLTS

FOOTING

GRAVEL

4x4 POST

METAL POST ANCHOR

Smart Tip

To extend the life of your deck, do not expose the porous end grain of wood balusters and posts.—D.S.

Deck Materials. For a deck, use rot-resistant wood, such as red cedar, cypress, or redwood, or pressure-treated lumber, which resists decay. Cedar and redwood are the two preferred choices for decks because they are strong and durable; both woods weather to a pleasing natural gray. However, while cedar and redwood are decay-resistant, they are vulnerable to rot in areas that remain warm and damp for extended periods. Some of the newer decking materials that are made from recycled materials and plastics are not harmed by water and do not produce splinters. In addition, they require little maintenance.

The cost will vary with the type of wood you choose. Least expensive is pressure-treated lumber. However, treated wood is more likely to split than naturally rot-resistant woods, and it is not as attractive as untreated wood.

An open-rail fence, opposite, provides a view of the harbor. The deck's design accommodates an old tree.

INCLUDE BUILT-IN SEATING AND STORAGE

YOU CAN SAVE SPACE and add to the interest of your deck or patio with built-in seating. If your design includes a railing, benches can be built into it. For a more comfortable back support, consider slanting the rail outward. If there are no railings, include separate benches, perhaps placing them along the edges of the deck. Add interest to a blank wall that adjoins the patio or deck by running a bench along its length. In addition to creating seating space, use the bench to display potted plants.

Benches can also break up large expanses of paving and help define activity areas. If possible, arrange the seating so that people can look at each other. If you run benches down adjoining sides, you'll have a corner where people can turn toward each other to converse.

Build seating that doubles as storage space. Instead of a bench seat resting on legs, build a weathertight storage box topped with a hinged lid. This chest becomes a place to keep toys, pool equipment, games, chair cushions, or extra towels.

Benches are a logical landing near a pool for wet towels and swimming gear.

PATHS AND THEIR DESIGN

Paths are meant to lead comfortably from one point to another but they are also an important part of the basic structure of a landscape, enhancing the composition. Like hedges or specimen trees, paths add to the sense of design and order in the landscape.

Path Surfaces

The type of surface for the path affects its appearance as well as the experience of walking on it. Gravel makes a lovely crunching sound when you walk on it, and it's adaptable to both informal and formal settings. Some

Smart Tip

Some materials, such as wood and certain types of stone, become slippery when wet, creating a potential hazard. Others, such as gravel and bark chips, should be contained with proper edges, and are not suited for use near the pool or spa.—D.S.

kinds of flagstone take on a beautiful sheen when they're wet. A wooden surface has more spring to it than stone or brick. A bark or pine-needle path through a woodland garden is in complete harmony with its surroundings. Some of the most charming paths are a mixture of materials.

Installing Paths

Whether your path surface is loose-laid brick or crushed quarry stone, a crazy pavement made of random-shaped flag- or field-stone, or a formal brick or stone path that is set with concrete and mortar, many of the steps for layout and building are the same. To estimate the amount of material you'll need for the path, lay out the path; measure the length and width; and then multiply the two numbers to get the square feet of your path. For curved paths, it may help to run a string the length of the path, following the curves, and then measure the string. It's easy to work out the number of bricks needed if they are a standard size. Stone can be more difficult. Let the experts at the quarry work out the amount of stone you'll need.

A bark path is an excellent choice in the natural setting of a garden—but not near the pool.

POSSIBLE MATERIALS FOR A GARDEN PATH

MATERIALS STRONGLY AFFECT the character of a path. Wood bark is perfect for woodland gardens. Flagstone is more structured but still gives the landscape a country look. Terra-cotta tile is effective in establishing a sense of the Southwest. Crushed oyster shells also impart a strong regional flavor and are one of the few ways to create a white path.

- Aggregate stone
- Bark (chipped or shredded)
- Brick or brick chips
- Ceramic tile
- Cobblestones
- Concrete paving blocks
- Crazy paving
- Fieldstone
- Flagstone
- Granite blocks
- Grass
- Gravel
- Interlocking pavers
- Marble
- Millstones
- Pebbles or cobbles set in mosaic pattern
- Pine needles
- Reconstituted stone
- Seashells (crushed)
- Terra-cotta tile
- Wood
- Wooden rounds

Aggregate Stone

Brick

Flagstone

Seashells

Grass

8

Around the Pool

CUTTING BRICK OR STONE

YOU MAY NEED only a partial brick or piece of stone to fit within the layout. Cut it to size with a chisel or brickset to score along the desired break line on all four sides. Set the scored brick on sand. Place a brickset along the scored line with its bevel away from the side of the finished cut. Rap sharply on the end of the brickset handle with a hammer.

To cut a piece of stone, after scoring it on the top and bottom, lay the stone across a support board, with the part to be removed hanging over the edge. Place a brickset on the score line, and hit the chisel handle sharply with a hammer. Turn the stone over, and repeat the process until the stone is cut. Wear safety glasses.

Installing a Loose-Laid Brick Path

Difficulty Level: Moderate

To create an informal path, install the bricks in a plain running bond pattern or set them in a more decorative arrangement, such as basket weave, herringbone, or diagonal herringbone.

If you need a partial brick, you can cut it to size. (See "Cutting Brick or Stone," at left.)

1 Excavate the path to 7 in. Line the path with perforated plastic sheeting to keep weeds down. In this picture, the deeper trench will bring water to a fountain that will be installed in the future.

4 Add a 1-in. layer of stone dust to the subbase. Then draw a board across it. Starting at the end of the path, lay the bricks. Place a spirit level over each row, and check both directions. Set the bricks with a rubber mallet (inset).

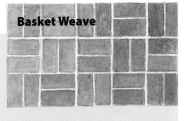

Running Bond

Basket Weave

Herringbone

Diagonal Herringbone

Don't forget: wear work gloves and safety goggles.

Tools and Materials: Shovel or spade, wheelbarrow, metal rake, string, spirit level, landscape fabric or perforated plastic sheeting, ³⁄₄-inch coarse gravel, retaining edge, edging spikes, stone dust, bricks, rubber mallet, builder's sand, broom, pressure-treated lumber.

8

Around the Pool

2 Apply a 4-in. layer of coarse ³⁄₄-in. gravel. Install a retaining edge. Stretch string along the length of the path to keep the edges level and straight. Secure the edging with pegs that fit into slots built into the metal strips (inset).

3 In spots where extra fill is required, such as on this slope, build a deeper edging out of pressure-treated lumber. Wedge the wooden edging into place with stakes hammered into the ground.

5 Sweep a medium-grade builder's sand over the surface of the bricks, moving the broom in different directions so that the bristles can work the sand into the narrow spaces between the bricks.

6 Remove or hose off the excess sand, revealing the brick pattern beneath. The finished, loose-laid path that is pictured here looks traditional without appearing rigid or formal.

LANDSCAPE LIGHTING

Outdoor lighting can transform night into an enchanting time, highlighting parts of the yard and pool area in new ways. Garden lights also prolong the time that you can be outdoors, especially in the transitional seasons of spring and autumn when the days are shorter but the temperature is still warm enough to be swimming or using the spa. In addition to the aesthetic benefits, outdoor lighting can make your property safer for walking around at night.

Installing a 120-volt garden lighting system, however, is an expensive and labor-intensive job that requires buried waterproof pipes. As with other electrical projects, strict safety codes must be followed. Installation of a 120-volt system is usually best left to professional electricians. Fortunately, there is an inexpensive alternative to 120-volt systems, called low-voltage outdoor lighting. The fixtures are available in a variety of styles and finishes that allow you to complement the architecture of your home. The lamps for low-voltage lighting commonly range between 25 and 50 watts.

Low-Voltage Lighting Systems

Low-voltage lights use only 12 volts of electricity instead of 120. You need to install a transformer to step down the 120-volt power to 12 volts. A typical six-light set uses less electricity than a 60-watt bulb, costing pennies per evening to operate. Best of all, most of the low-voltage systems are reasonably inexpensive and easy to install.

The only hard part of installing low-voltage lights is deciding where you want to locate the lights and which of the many effects you want to create. There are kits avail-

Edge lighting accentuates the pool's shape and illuminates the walk around its perimeter.

able designed for specific purposes. Check them out to help you make your decisions. For the sake of economy and tidiness, try to minimize the amount of wire you need. Once you're ready to connect the wires, the job literally takes minutes.

This low-profile flare light casts light downward and around its base area to accent a special plant. You can use several of them to light a path.

This low-profile well light casts light upward to draw attention to an evergreen shrub. The hood can be turned 360 deg. to change the focus.

Installing Low-Voltage Lights

Difficulty Level: Easy

Lay out the wire in a direct route, which avoids crossing the wire back over itself or making tight, twisty turns, following the manufacturer's instructions. Be careful not to exceed the prescribed number of lights for each circuit. The transformer must be plugged into a properly in-

stalled GFCI-protected outdoor outlet. If you don't have an outdoor outlet, have one installed by a professional electrician following local codes.

Tools and Materials: lights, fixtures, wires, transformer box, measuring tape to mark the spacing between lights, wire cutters (with a stripper), pliers, insulated screwdriver.

1 Position your low-voltage lighting system along the specified landscaping feature. Using the attached ground spikes, install the system by driving the spikes into the ground.

2 Lay the low-voltage cable that connects the lights in a trench that is at least 6 in. deep. Clip the wire leads from each light fixture to the cable. Do not cover the trench yet.

3 Following the manufacturer's installation guidelines, connect the low-voltage wires to the 12-volt step-down transformer. Use an insulated screwdriver for this part of the job.

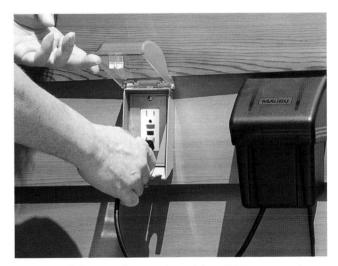

4 Install the transformer alongside a GFCI-protected outlet. Plug in the transformer and test the lights. If necessary, go back and recheck the connections. Once everything is in working order, refill the trench.

RETAINING WALLS

Retaining walls have a double purpose. In addition to being ornamental, they hold back soil to convert a slope into level areas or terraces. Terracing a steep hillside is a time-honored way to transform unused land into broad level "steps" for garden beds or paved areas. Because retaining walls must be able to support the added weight of tons of soil, they must be even more stable than freestanding garden walls. As with garden walls, the footings of retaining walls should extend below the frost line where freezing is an issue.

Smart Tip

Before you begin building, check with local authorities and secure all required permits. Many communities require that you hire a professional engineer to design any retaining wall that will be more than 4 feet tall.—D.S.

Provide drainage for a retaining wall so that water doesn't build up behind it. Waterlogged soil is very heavy and unstable. Drainage can be furnished by building weep holes into the wall, or by running perforated pipe behind the wall before it is backfilled with soil.

Materials for Retaining Walls

Choose a building material that is suitable for the site and creates the overall effect you want. Materials for retaining walls include wood, precast blocks, brick, and concrete.

Wooden Retaining Walls. Generally wooden walls are the easiest and least expensive way to tame a slope. They usually look less formal than terraces walled with stone or brick. Wood tends to survive longer in drier climates than wet ones and on well-drained slopes. On a large slope, where the wall must support tons of earth, you must use heavy lumber such as landscape timbers. To delay rotting, choose either pressure-treated lumber or wood that is resistant to decay, such as redwood, cedar, or

A stone retaining wall permits the creation of a flower garden next to the pool on this sloped site.

Interlocking concrete-block walls are relatively easy to install following manufacturers' directions.

cypress. If you want to avoid digging deep holes for support posts, you can use deadman braces to give structural strength to a timber retaining wall. Deadmen should be installed along your wall in the second or third course from the bottom and in the second course from the top.

Brick, Concrete Block, or Poured Concrete Walls. Masonry retaining walls are usually reinforced with steel rebar and are the strongest you can install.

Retaining walls that are constructed of brick or block must stand on a concrete footing. Footings should be the same thickness as the wall and twice as wide as they are thick. If the frostline runs from several inches to several feet below ground level, build a below-ground wall of concrete on top of the footing and then build the retaining wall on top of the concrete wall at ground level.

Interlocking Concrete-Block Walls. Many interlocking blocks are cast to look like natural stone. Most systems interlock by means of pins, clips, or joints cast into the block itself. Once a footing or gravel bed is placed, the blocks can be fastened together. Usually, blocks interlock so that each horizontal course is stepped back from the one beneath to create a better angle. Systems include corner and cap blocks.

8

Around the Pool

INTERLOCKING BLOCK WALL

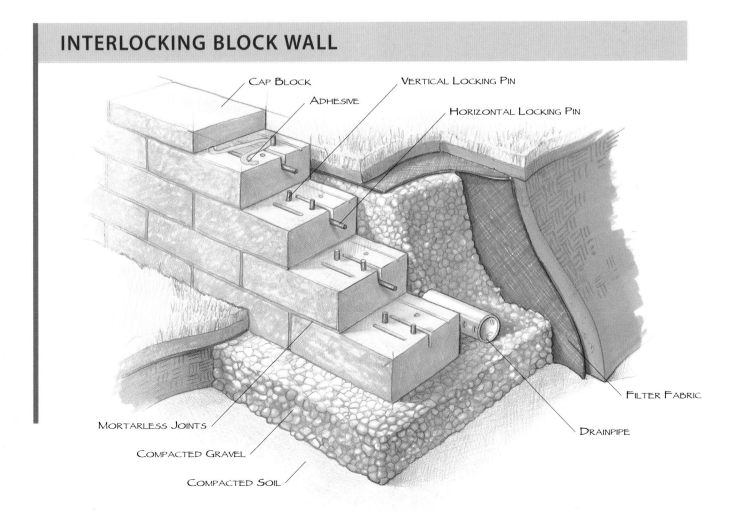

CAP BLOCK

ADHESIVE

VERTICAL LOCKING PIN

HORIZONTAL LOCKING PIN

FILTER FABRIC

MORTARLESS JOINTS

DRAINPIPE

COMPACTED GRAVEL

COMPACTED SOIL

PLANTINGS

Plantings around a pool relieve the starkness of paving and add much-needed height to a predominantly horizontal landscape feature. They can be ornamental; trees can pro-vide shady relief from the hot afternoon sun.

Bear in mind, however, that swimming pools can create specific challenges for plants, such as withstanding chlorinated water. You must avoid plants with invasive roots that could crack the walls of an in-ground pool or spa.

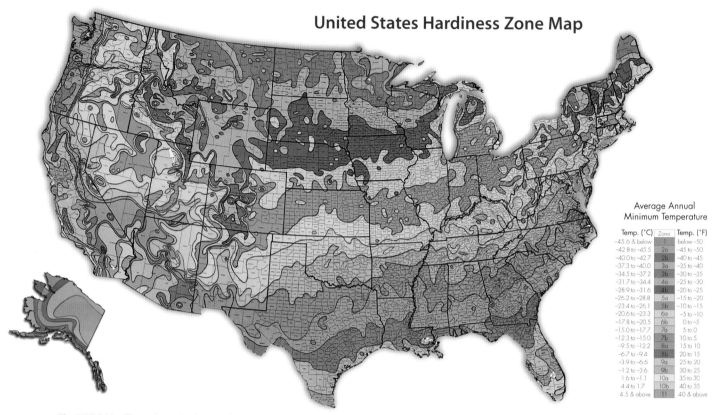

United States Hardiness Zone Map

Average Annual Minimum Temperature

Temp. (°C)	Zone	Temp. (°F)
-45.6 & below	1	below -50
-42.8 to -45.5	2a	-45 to -50
-40.0 to -42.7	2b	-40 to -45
-37.3 to -40.0	3a	-35 to -40
-34.5 to -37.2	3b	-30 to -35
-31.7 to -34.4	4a	-25 to -30
-28.9 to -31.6	4b	-20 to -25
-26.2 to -28.8	5a	-15 to -20
-23.4 to -26.1	5b	-10 to -15
-20.6 to -23.3	6a	-5 to -10
-17.8 to -20.5	6b	0 to -5
-15.0 to -17.7	7a	5 to 0
-12.3 to -15.0	7b	10 to 5
-9.5 to -12.2	8a	15 to 10
-6.7 to -9.4	8b	20 to 15
-3.9 to -6.6	9a	25 to 20
-1.2 to -3.6	9b	30 to 25
1.6 to -1.1	10a	35 to 30
4.4 to 1.7	10b	40 to 35
4.5 & above	11	40 & above

The USDA Hardiness Map divides North America into 11 zones according to average minimum winter temperatures. Hardiness zones are used to identify regions to which plants are suited based on their cold tolerance, which is what "hardiness" means. Many factors, such as elevation and moisture level, come into play when determining whether a plant is suitable for your region. Local climates may vary from what is shown on this map. Contact your local Cooperative Extension Service for recommendations for your area.

Canada Hardiness Zone Map

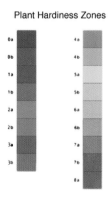

Plant Hardiness Zones

0a	4a
0b	4b
1a	5a
1b	5b
2a	6a
2b	6b
3a	7a
3b	7b
	8a

Canada's Plant Hardiness Zone Map outlines the different zones in Canada where various types of trees, shrubs, and flowers will most likely survive. It is based on the average climactic conditions of each area. The hardiness map is divided into nine major zones: the harshest is 0 and the mildest is 8. Relatively few plants are suited to zone 0. Subzones (e.g., 4a or 4b, 5a or 5b) are also noted in the map legend. These subzones are most familiar to Canadian gardeners. Some significant local factors, such as microtopography, amount of shelter, and subtle local variations in snow cover, are too small to be captured on the map. Year-to-year variations in weather and gardening techniques can also have a significant impact on plant survival in any particular location.

SELECTING POOLSIDE PLANTS

- **Poolside plants should be tidy.** Avoid plants that will drop leaves, petals, or fruit, as well as plants with tiny leaves that can clog the filter. Choose trees that don't have invasive or extensive roots, which can cause the pool decking to heave.

- **Choose chemical-tolerant plants.** Poolside plants are likely to have chlorinated water splashed onto them. A good solution is to choose plants that are less sensitive to pool chemicals. Some of the many plants suitable to grow near swimming pools are ornamental grasses, treasure flowers, daylilies, junipers, and Atlas cedars.

- **Use low-maintenance plants.** When designing your poolside plantings, keep the beds as low-maintenance as possible so that you can spend your time swimming rather than tending plants that require high care levels. Avoid plants such as roses, which often require a program of regular spraying to look their best; you wouldn't want those chemicals in the pool water.

- **Try potted plants instead of beds.** Invest in several tubs or urns that are large enough to hold a small tree or shrub.

- **Exercise caution with fragrant plants,** as they often attract bees.

- **Include drainage in the pool decking.** Whether you decide to include beds right up to the pool or place them around the periphery, make sure that the decking has a good drainage system that will direct water away from the house and the beds.

8

Around the Pool

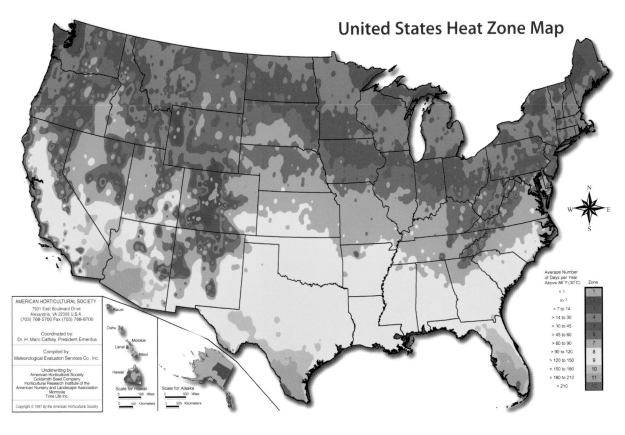

United States Heat Zone Map

The **American Horticultural Society Heat-Zone Map** divides the United States into 12 zones based on the average annual number of days a region's temperatures climb above 86°F (30°C), the temperature at which the cellular proteins of plants begin to experience injury. Introduced in 1998, the AHS Heat-Zone Map holds significance, especially for gardeners in southern and transitional zones. Nurseries, growers, and other plant sources will gradually begin listing both cold hardiness and heat tolerance zones for plants, including grass plants. Using the USDA Plant Hardiness map, which can help determine a plant's cold tolerance, and the AHS Heat-Zone Map, gardeners will be able to safely choose plants that tolerate their region's lowest and highest temperatures.

Soil Considerations

Before you start buying plants and digging holes, analyze the soil in your yard. The basis of a healthy garden is its soil. Pests may annoy and diseases may intrude, but in most cases if the plants are growing in good soil, they will be resilient enough to overcome these travails. On the other hand, if the soil is missing a key nutrient or if the pH is off for a particular plant, the plant will begin to fail and will then be vulnerable to a host of pests and diseases. Intense soil amendment is particularly important if you are planting perennials, annuals, or vegetables. If you are planting trees and shrubs, which have root systems that will delve far deeper than you can amend, your best chance for success is to choose native plants.

pH Levels. The pH level is a measure of how much hydrogen is in the soil, which in turn affects how available nutrients are to your plants. Most ornamental plants, vegetables, and herbs do best in soil with a pH between 5 and 7. Woodland plants, including rhododendrons, azaleas, ferns, and astilbes do best in slightly acidic, or "sour," soil (below 5), while plants such as clematis prefer alkaline, or "sweet," soil with a pH of 8 or higher. Turf grass does best with a pH of 5.8 to 6.6. Soil pH figures are always given in a range. But be aware that pH figures change exponentially. If your soil is at the extreme ends of the range or outside of the suggested figure, you will most likely need to add amendments.

Smart Tip

Most garden centers sell pH test kits with which you can test your own soil. However, you must also find out whether the soil is sandy, clay, loam, or some combination of the three. This is important information because it affects the amount of amendments needed.—D.S.

A lush setting for a pool includes a variety of trees, shrubs, and flowering perennials and annuals.

Acidic and Alkaline Soil. Typically, parts of the country that receive plenty of rain, such as the eastern third of the United States and Canada, tend to have acidic soil. Dry regions, such as the southwestern United States, usually have alkaline soil. However, don't assume that the soil on your property necessarily matches what is typical for the region where you live. Parts of your property could have significantly different pH levels if the soil was heavily fertilized, if it's located at the end of a flood runoff, or if mineral substances ever leached into the soil. If you are new to the property, it's a good idea to test several samples of the soil.

Nutrient Analysis. A nutrient analysis requires serious chemistry. It's usually best to pay the fee for a soil analysis from your Cooperative Extension Service or from a commercial laboratory that includes information on soil pH as well as a breakdown of the soil's nutrients. The report will include recommendations on the amounts and types of amendments and fertilizers needed. Nitrogen is the one basic nutrient that usually isn't included, because nitrogen levels in soil fluctuate daily, making that measurement meaningless.

Soil Texture

In addition to having an appropriate pH and blend of nutrients, your soil should have a good structure, with spaces for air and water. Structure can be improved, although the texture—clay, sand, or loam—will not change. The easiest way for you to improve the structure of your landscape's soil is to add organic matter. To determine the texture of your soil, simply squeeze a handful in your palm and study its structure.

Clay Soil. Heavy clay soil will form a tight ball. Clay is composed of extremely fine particles that pack together closely, so water drains slowly. Clay soil contains very little oxygen. Because this soil is dense, roots have a hard time pushing through it.

Sandy Soil. Sandy soil, by contrast, will not hold together at all. Its loose, coarse particles allow space for lots of oxygen and easy root growth. Water can drain easily, but it can also leach out essential nutrients. Another disadvantage of sandy soil is that it dries out quickly; water drains so easily that it disappears before plants can use it.

An informal landscape of easy-care grasses and shrubs, above, complements some lifestyles.

Flowering shrubs, below, require the right soil conditions for their particular region.

Silty Soil. Silty soil feels silky or even soapy. Silt is sedimentary material that is coarser than clay but still comprised of fine particles. It compacts easily.

Loam. The ideal soil is a rich loam balanced in its composition of clay, silt, and sand particles, and containing plenty of organic materials such as humus or manure. When you squeeze loam in your hand, it will form a shape but then crumble easily. That indicates that loam retains enough water for plant roots, but it still drains freely and is well aerated.

Determine Its Purpose

Trees and shrubs are excellent for providing mass in your landscape. They can be useful to screen an unattractive view, lower noise levels, cut the wind, and provide shade. If you want to plant a tree or shrub as a focal point in the center of a lawn, you can choose a large spreading specimen that will become ever more spectacular as it grows. But if you want to plant a tree along a driveway or patio, don't choose one with invasive roots. For example, weeping willow roots search for water, even boring through pipes, and can heave up a concrete walkway or crack a house foundation. So don't plant one near the pool or near the buried piping of the circulation system.

TREES SUITABLE FOR PATIOS

TREES PLANTED next to a patio or in a planter in the middle of the area provide welcome shade. Choose small, tidy specimens with non-invasive roots such as the following:

Acer griseum (paperbark maple), **Zones 4–8**
Acer palmatum (Japanese maple), **Zones 6–8**
Albizia julibrissin (mimosa), **Zones 6–10**
Betula (birch), zones vary with species
Carpinus betulus (European hornbeam),
 Zones 4–7
C. caroliniana (American hornbeam), **Zones 2–9**
Cercis canadensis (eastern redbud), **Zones 5–9**
Cercis occidentalis (California or western
 redbud), **Zones 6–10**
Chinonanthus retusus (Chinese fringe tree),
 Zones 6–10
Chinonanthus virginicus (fringe tree), **Zones 5–9**
Cornus florida (flowering dogwood), **Zones 5–8**
Cornus kousa (Kousa dogwood), **Zones 5–8**
Cornus x rutgersens (Stellar series), **Zones 5–8**
Crataegus laevigata (English hawthorn),
 Zones 5–8
Jacaranda mimosifolia (jacaranda), **Zone 10**

Include shrubs and even small trees in flower borders to provide interest in winter and to anchor the design. Border a bed with a low-growing shrub such as dwarf boxwood or Santolina to frame and give definition to the plantings. Line a path with scented shrubs such as lavender, or plant a bulky shrub at the curve of a winding path to obscure the view around a corner. For a patio tree, you want one that will provide shade as well as visual interest such as pretty flowers, fruit, foliage, and/or bark. Stay away from messy trees that shed regularly or drop sticky fruit or sap, creating the need for frequent cleanup on paved surfaces.

Consider Unusual Shapes

Don't overlook the importance of key plants with a bold or unusual shape. A tree or shrub that naturally grows in a striking form, such as the pagoda dogwood (*Cornus alternifolia*) or a spectacular specimen tree, such as a monumental chestnut or beech tree, makes a fascinating focal point, giving structure and visual direction to the overall design. If your property already has a significant, established tree, try to plan your landscape and pool to emphasize that asset.

Keep trees and bushes that shed leaves or flowers away from the pool area.

TREES FOR THE LANDSCAPE

TOO OFTEN A YOUNG TREE OR SHRUB is planted close to a structure with no allowance made for its growth. Some of the plants listed here may technically be shrubs, but because of their mature height, they are listed as trees.

Small Trees (up to 30 feet tall)

Acer japonicum (Japanese maple), **Zones 6–9**

    A. tataricum ssp. *ginnala* (Amur maple), **Zones 3–7**

Amelanchier laevis (Allegheny serviceberry), **Zones 4–9**

Arbutus unedo (strawberry tree), **Zones 7–9**

Cercis canadensis (eastern redbud), **Zones 4–9**

Chionanthus retusus (Chinese fringe tree), **Zones 6–8**

Cornus florida (flowering dogwood), **Zones 5–9**

Franklinia alatamaha (Franklin tree), **Zones 5–8 or 9**

Magnolia x soulangiana (saucer magnolia), **Zones 5–9**

Magnolia stellata (star magnolia), **Zones 4–8**

Malus sp. (flowering crab apple), zones vary with species

Oxydendrum arboreum (sourwood), **Zones 5–9**

Prunus x blireana (flowering plum), **Zones 5–8**

Styrax japonicum (Japanese snowbell), **Zones 5–9**

Medium to Large Trees (30 feet and taller)

Acer rubrum (red maple), **Zones 3–9**

Acer saccharinum (silver maple), **Zones 3–9**

Albizia julibrissin (silk tree or mimosa), **Zones 6–10**

Cercidiphyllum japonicum (Katsura tree), **Zones 4–8**

Fraxinus pennsylvanica (green ash), **Zones 3–9**

Ginkgo biloba (ginkgo, maidenhair tree), **Zones 4–9**

Gleditsia triacanthos (honey locust), **Zones 4–9**

Gymnocladus dioica (Kentucky coffee tree), **Zones 4–9**

Halesia tetraptera (Carolina silver bell), **Zones 5–9**

Koelreuteria paniculata (varnish tree), **Zones 5–9**

Lagerstroemia indica (crape myrtle), **Zones 7–9**

Nyssa sylvatica (sour gum), **Zones 4–9**

Parrotia persica (Persian ironwood), **Zones 5–8**

Sophora japonica (pagoda tree), **Zones 4–9**

Stewartia pseudocamellia, **Zones 5–8**

Tilia cordata (littleleaf linden), **Zones 4–7**

Zelkova serrata (Japanese zelkova), **Zones 5–9**

Tucked away at the bottom of a hillside, this pool area, top, is a secluded getaway.

Fruit trees, above, add color and scent to a lap pool located in a warm, sunny climate.

Wild spaces, below, can serve as a backdrop for your pool or spa.

SHRUBS FOR THE LANDSCAPE

Shrubs with Attractive Flowers

Camellia japonica, and *C. sasanqua,* **Zones 7–10**

Chaenomeles (flowering quince), **Zones 5–9**

Cytisus x praecox (Warminster broom), **Zones 7–9**

Daphne cneorum (garland flower), **Zones 4–9**

Hamamelis x intermedia (witch hazel), **Zones 5–9**

Hydrangea macrophylla, **Zones 6–10**

Hypericum sp. (St. John's wort), zones vary with species

Kalmia latifolia (mountain laurel), **Zones 4–9**

Kerria japonica (Japanese rose or kerria), **Zones 4–9**

Lagerstroemia indica (crape myrtle), **Zones 7–9**

Philadelphus species and cultivars (sweet mock orange),
    Zones 4–8

Pieris japonica (Japanese andromeda), **Zones 6–8**

Potentilla fruticosa (shrubby cinquefoil), **Zones 2–7**

Prunus triloba (flowering almond), **Zones 3–8**

Spiraea japonica (Japanese spirea), **Zones 4–8**

Viburnum species (viburnum), zones vary with species

Weigela florida (weigela), **Zones 5–9**

Shrubs with Attractive Berries

Berberis darwinii, **Zones 8–10**

Berberis wilsoniae (Wilson barberry), **Zones 7–10**

Callicarpa americana (beautyberry), **Zones 7–10**

Callicarpa bodinieri (beautyberry), **Zones 6–8**, good
    to **Zone 10** in West

Cotoneaster lucidus (hedge cotoneaster), **Zones 4–7**

Cotoneaster salicifolius (willowleaf cotoneaster),
    Zones 6–8 in the East; **6–10** in the West

Euonymus alata (burning bush), **Zones 4–9**

Ilex species (holly), zones vary with species

Mahonia aquifolium (Oregon grape), **Zones 5–9**

Mahonia bealei, **Zones 7–9**

Nandina domestica (heavenly bamboo), **Zones 7–10**

Photinia serratifolia (Chinese photinia), **Zones 7–9**
    in the East; **7–10** in the West

Pyracantha coccinea (scarlet firethorn), **Zones 6–9**

Rhus typhina (staghorn sumac), **Zones 4–8**

Viburnum species (viburnum), zones vary with species

Plantings intermingle with this pool's free-form rock surround, top.

Manicured hedges, above, add a slightly formal feeling to this pool area.

Seasonal color brings added appeal to the landscaped area, below.

Planting Trees and Shrubs

Today, experts suggest digging a hole just deep enough to hold the plant. That way the soil won't settle.

Evidence suggests that trees and shrubs grow better if they are planted directly into the native soil rather than into amended soil. Ultimately you want the tree's roots to extend well beyond the original hole. If the soil in the hole is much richer than the surrounding native soil, the roots will avoid growing beyond that luxurious environment. The result is that they become rootbound in their own hole. These facts make it all the more important to choose trees and shrubs that are suited to the native soil. You'll experience nothing but frustration if you select a tree or shrub that prefers sandy soil and plant it in clay, or plant a shrub that needs acidic soil (a low pH) in alkaline soil. If your soil is heavy, plant trees and shrubs about 2 inches above the level it grew in the nursery field. Look for the soil-line stain on the trunk for a guide.

Some site clearing was necessary here, but many old trees were retained as a natural backdrop for this pool.

Smart Tip

Many deciduous trees and shrubs are available in early spring as bare-root stock. This is an economical way to buy plants because they are lighter and less bulky for nurseries to ship. If you don't have time to plant them in their proper place, plant them temporarily in a shady, wind-protected location with the trunk tilted on a sharp diagonal to discourage rooting. Bare-root trees and shrubs are still dormant. Until they start sprouting, water only if the soil becomes dry. Once the active growing season begins, water as you would any new plant.

Conventional wisdom used to dictate pruning back trees at planting time to create a balance between roots and foliage. More recent evidence shows that the extra foliage produces hormones that encourage root regeneration. If there are any broken branches, remove them; leave the rest alone.—D.S.

8

Around the Pool

Planting Balled-and-Burlapped Stock

Difficulty Level: Easy

Trees and shrubs that are grown at the nursery are often balled and burlapped after they are dug from the ground. This means that the roots are enclosed in a ball of original soil and the ball is wrapped in burlap and tied together. Like any newly planted tree or shrub, balled-and-burlapped plants need extra care the first year or so. Be especially careful when watering. Many balled-and-burlapped plants are field-grown in heavy clay soil, which absorbs water slowly.

If your native soil is lighter, it will take in water much more quickly. When you water, make sure that the root ball is getting properly saturated. If in doubt about whether you have watered enough, gently insert a dry wooden stick, such as a paint stirrer, into the soil. Pull it out after an hour or so. If the soil is moist enough, the stick will have absorbed moisture and will have become slightly darker.

Tools and Materials: Shovel, scissors (or wire clipper if the rootball is contained in a cage), tarp, water, plant, mulch.

1 Remove enough soil to make a hole that is about the same depth as the root ball and twice as wide. Put the soil on the tarp. The bottom of the hole should be covered with firm, undisturbed soil.

2 Hold the plant at the base of the trunk, and place it in the hole to check the depth, making sure that the crown is slightly above ground level. Add water until it pools in the bottom of the hole.

3 Untie the wrapping (or cut the cage off) and remove the burlap from the plant. Fill the hole with soil from the tarp, and tamp it down with your foot to eliminate air holes and stabilize the plant.

4 Build a shallow moat around the trunk. Fill the moat with water, and let it dissipate. Put several inches of mulch around the trunk, but do not pack the mulch right up against the trunk.

HEDGES

Hedges are invaluable in the landscape to screen unwanted views or high winds, to define garden spaces, to frame vistas, and to serve as a backdrop to borders or decorative elements such as sculpture. Traditionally, we think of a hedge as a neatly pruned row of one species of plant. While that approach creates a tidy, uniform look that is ideal for informal settings, there is no rule against combining different shrubs, even flowering ones, with a variety of leaf colors and textures to create a hedge with a tapestry effect. You can either shear the plants for a tailored look or allow the shrubs to billow in their natural form for a soft, informal backdrop.

CONIFERS FOR HEDGES

Cephalotaxus fortunei (Chinese plum yew), **Zones 7–9,** slow growing

Chamaecyparis lawsoniana (Lawson false cypress or Port Orford cedar), **Zones 5–9,** medium growth rate

C. x Cupressocyparis leylandii (Leyland cypress), **Zones 6–10,** very fast growing

Cupressus macrocarpa (Monterey cypress), **Zones 7–9,** growth rate varies with cultivars

Juniperus chinensis (Chinese juniper), **Zones 4–10,** slow to medium growth rate

Juniperus scopulorum (Rocky Mountain juniper), **Zones 4–10,** slow-growing

Podocarpus macrophylla (southern yew), **Zones 7–10,** slow growing

Pseudotsuga menziesii (Douglas fir), **Zones 4–7,** medium growth rate

Taxus baccata (English yew), **Zones 5–8** in the East; **5–10** in the West, slow growing

Thuja plicata (western red cedar), **Zones 6–7,** growth varies with cultivars

Tsuga canadensis (Canada hemlock), **Zones 4–7,** medium growth rate

Smart Tip

The natural inclination when choosing a shrub for a hedge is to choose a plant that will grow as fast as possible. While the quick results are gratifying, the downside is that faster-growing plants tend to be shorter-lived.—

Consider the Rate of Growth

Slow-growing yew and boxwood are the traditional shrubs used for hedges. Boxwoods need only occasional pruning to keep them within bounds. With regular pruning, some conifers can be kept the size of medium to large shrubs.

As you consider all of the wonderful plants available for creating hedges, weigh the pros and cons of the faster-growing hedging plants versus slower-growing plants with greater longevity. To work out the number of plants you need, first find out the expected mature width of the shrub.

Boxwood interplanted with columnar yew (*Taxus*) is a classic-looking, no-maintenance hedge.

Planting a Hedge

Planting a hedge takes a little more care than simply putting in one or two plants at random because you want the plants to follow the line of the hedge and to be spaced properly, especially if your aim is privacy. In theory, you should simply have to divide the length of the hedge by the projected width of each plant to find out how many plants to buy. However, you can't count on a plant ever growing to its optimal size. If soil, light, or moisture conditions are not ideal, the shrub may take years to fulfill its potential—or it may never reach it. Because you definitely want the plants to touch and even overlap to make an unbroken hedge, reduce the average expected width of each plant by about one third, and then do the division. Commercial landscapers typically plant shrubs much closer together than necessary to get a filled-in hedge more quickly. As a homeowner, you probably want to compromise between using a minimum number of plants and jamming them in tightly for an instant effect.

A mixed-planting hedge, above, is a garden in itself. Some of the shrubs here include roses, forsythia, and yew.

A row of hedges flanking a lattice gate creates an informal entry into the garden and pool area, below.

Planting Container-Grown Hedge Plants

Difficulty Level: Easy

First mark out the line where you want the hedge. If you are making a curved hedge, use a hose to mark out the line you want, and leave it in place until you are ready to dig. Once you have your plants, position them along the line, making the spaces between each as even as possible. Remember to allow growing space for the plants at each end; set these at half the spacing distance in from the desired end of your hedge. Mulch along the row with an organic material such as straw, shredded bark, or shredded leaves. The mulch will have to be 4 to 6 inches deep to make it effective in minimizing evaporation and as a deterrent against weeds.

Tools and Materials: Hose, string, tape measure, stakes, shovel, tarp, plants, mulch, water.

1 Run string between stakes along the hedge line. Either dig a trench beneath the string or position the plants precisely using a tape measure. Dig a hole for each plant. Water each plant, and slide it out of its container.

2 Break up the root ball with your fingers or with a few vertical cuts. Position the plant straight in the hole, and backfill until the crown of the plant is at the same depth as it was growing in the pot.

3 Water each plant thoroughly as you dig it in. Allow the water to disperse in the hole, and water again. Apply an organic mulch around each plant and between plants along the row.

4 Check again to make sure that the plants are positioned in a straight line. Dig new holes if necessary, and replant any shrubs that are out of line. Pull up the stakes and string.

PONDS

Even if your yard is small, you may be able to find a spot for an attractive water feature, such as a pond. But you can't expect to simply dig a hole in the ground and have it hold water. You'll need to provide a watertight foundation, which you can do with a proper liner or shell.

Flexible Pond Liners

The big selling point of flexible liners is their design malleability. Flexible liners are also relatively inexpensive and easy for the do-it-yourselfer to install. Naturally, flexible liners cost more. However, they come in stock sizes ranging from about 5 x 5 feet to 30 x 50 feet. Some manufacturers offer custom sizes, which are priced by the square foot. By joining the edges of the sheets with a special seam sealer, you can make a pond of virtually any size or shape. Because flexible liners are susceptible to punctures, you have to cushion them with an underlayment of some kind. Most water-garden suppliers offer a tough, flexible underlayment material specifically designed for use with pond liners; you can also buy liners that are bonded with underlayment material.

Preformed Pond Shells

Pond shells may be made of rigid or semirigid materials that are premolded to a specific shape and are also easy to install yourself. Although they come in an array of sizes, shapes, and depths, they won't give you the design choices that a flexible liner does. They are generally more expensive for their size but are also more durable and puncture-proof. Shells can last from 5 to 50 years depending on their composition, thickness, quality, and installation conditions. The thickest shells ($1/4$ inch or more) can be installed aboveground with little support around the sides, provided the bottom rests on a firm and level base.

Other Options

A concrete pond can last a lifetime if properly installed but will crack and leak almost immediately if it is not. If you decide to use concrete anyway, have the pond installed by a masonry contractor familiar with local building codes and this sort of construction in your particular climate.

Edgings

Pond edgings are typically rock, other masonry materials, or wood. The edging hides the rim, visually defines the pond perimeter, and keeps the surrounding soil from

Informal ponds, below left, give you the most design latitude.

Poured-concrete ponds, below right, require expert masonry skills to install properly.

A pond, opposite, can provide beauty, tranquility, and a harmonious linkage to nature.

washing into the water. Plan for the edging to overhang the pond by a few inches so that it hides the liner.

Pond Kits. Some manufacturers offer complete pond kits. The kits are easy to install but usually limited in size.

Adding Plants and Fish

Before adding plants or fish to a pond, test the water. Pond dealers, garden suppliers, and pet shops sell test kits.

Once the water conditions are right, you can safely introduce plants and critters.

Filters. If your goal is a small ornamental pond with a few plants and fish and you don't mind slightly clouded water, you may not need a filter. Otherwise, you will need some kind of filter (and a pump). Consult a specialist, such as a pond dealer or someone at a water-garden center, to get advice about what's suitable for your pond.

WATERFALLS

Some people want to add movement and sound to their pools or outdoor living environment through waterfalls, streams, fountains, or some combination of these.

For moving water, you will need a pump that is the right size for your project. Consult a specialist at a water-garden store before making a purchase. Just remember that the least-expensive pumps usually have the shortest lifespan and tend to clog easily.

Shaping a Waterfall

Keep a waterfall in scale with your pool or pond. A small trickle in a large pool won't be very dramatic, nor will it be effective at recirculating and oxygenating the water, which is necessary for maintaining aquatic plants and fish. But a large cascade gushing into a small pond will churn up sediment and make the environment nearly impossible for plants and fish as well.

For a wide, thin curtain of water, use smooth, flat flagstones. Or to produce a gushing sound, direct the water

designs. Informal styles are shaped to simulate natural rock. Formal preformed waterfalls are usually smaller versions of square or rectangular preformed ponds, with the addition of a built-in lip or spillway.

Fiberglass and plastic courses are lightweight and inexpensive, but the sizes and designs are limited. Preformed watercourses made of concrete or reconstituted stone are more realistic-looking, but they are heavier and, for practical purposes, limited to only a few square feet.

Designing a Stream

For some people a trickling rivulet is more picturesque than ocean waves. Nature usually arranges streams into a series of short, fairly flat sections separated by low falls or cascades. You'll need a pond or pool to feed your stream, unless you bury a water tank to take its place. A stream must be level to retain some water even when the pump is off. Alternating between wet and dry conditions can damage foundation materials. A stream that holds some water at all times also looks more realistic.

To prevent water loss between rocks or other edging, artificial waterfalls and streams are lined. In addition to a liner, they need underlayment material to cover the entire watercourse.

The sight and sound of a waterfall, opposite, can add to your outdoor enjoyment.

Creating a successful watercourse, above, is a mix of art and engineering.

Streams with straight or parallel channels enhance formal gardens, below right.

through a narrow gap between large boulders. Creating a hollow space behind the falls will amplify and echo the sound of falling water. While the lips of informal falls are formed from naturalistic materials with irregular shapes, those of formal waterfalls can be brick, tile, flagstone, or landscaping ties. Some formal designs incorporate a sheet of clear acrylic to create a wide, nearly transparent curtain of water. The plastic itself is all but invisible when the falls are in operation.

Preformed Waterfalls. Most companies that make preformed fiberglass or plastic ponds also sell preformed waterfall runs or courses of the same material. They are installed much like preformed rigid pond shells. The units consist of one or more basins with built-in cascades and a lower lip that empties into the pond. You can combine two or more short watercourses to produce a longer run, with each unit emptying into the one below it.

Preformed waterfalls come in informal as well as formal

FOUNTAINS

Fountains bring your pool or landscape to life with movement and sound. There are many types on today's market. To decide which one is best for you, consider style, sound, and size, as well as the other landscape and architectural elements on your property. If it will fit in your pond, keep in mind its effects on your plants and fish. You can also enjoy a stand-alone fountain that contains its own pump and catch basin; you provide electricity and just add water.

Types of Fountains

Fountains of all styles come in two basic types: *spray fountains* and *statuary fountains*.

Installing Spray Fountains. A spray fountain consists of a nozzle or ring attached to the outer pipe of a pump at or above the pond or pool's water level. Most spray fountains come as complete kits that contain a molded plastic nozzle, a pump, various fittings, and a flow-control valve that allows you to adjust spray height. Some kits contain several spray heads. Other kits come with a tee fitting and a diverter, which you'll need to attach another feature such as a waterfall or a filter. As with other components of water features, you get what you pay for. High-quality nozzles can be disassembled for

Wall fountains may be classical, above, or contemporary in style.

Self-contained fountains, below left, look natural pouring into a freeform pond or basin.

Spray fountains, opposite, with showy geysers are visually effective.

cleaning, for example. Nozzles with small holes clog easily and require frequent cleaning, which involves hosing it off or brushing it with an old toothbrush.

Installing Statuary Fountains. Most statuary fountains are made of precast concrete and may be finished to look like other material, such as alabaster or bronze. Some of them are sold separately from pumps and pedestals. Others are complete self-contained units with precast reservoir bowls and integrated, preplumbed pump and filter systems.

A wall fountain usually spills water through statuary, such as a mask or decorative plaque, that falls into a basin that hides the pump. The best location for a wall fountain is in a freestanding wall that allows you to run the plumbing behind it. If this is not practical, you could build out an existing wall using similar material. Mount the fountain on the new surface, and run the pipe behind it.

design ideas for pools and spas

A masonry wall, right, provides privacy and serves as a backdrop for plantings and distinctive water features.

A pergola, below, provides dappled shade to this pool deck. Note how it protects those in the spa from the full effects of the sun.

The curves of the pool, opposite top, are highlighted by the graceful shape of the low-growing hedge.

Surrounding your pool with trees and shrubs, opposite bottom, creates a soothing, garden-like feel, but be prepared for the maintenance responsibilities.

pools and spas

design ideas for

Even a small yard, opposite top, will benefit from a pool and its surrounding deck. The pool, deck, and yard must be in proportion to one another.

Include nature in your pool landscaping designs, opposite bottom. These large native rocks help anchor the pool stair.

Think of the pool as an integral part of the landscape, above, rather than as an object to surround with plants and patios.

This unusual water feature, left, is part of a larger landscape design. The shelf can hold potted water plants.

design ideas for pools and spas

A covered eating area, right, complements the pool and spa area beyond. The overhead structure helps delineate the area.

Use plantings, natural stone, and water features, as shown below, to soften the edges of a large pool.

Spouting fountain-type inlet heads, opposite top, serve to recirculate water back to the pool and provide an interesting accent.

For reduced maintenance, keep trees, shrubs, and lawns well back from the sides of the pool, opposite bottom.

CHAPTER 9

USING YOUR POOL AND SPA SAFELY

Worry-Free Fun

Everyone agrees that safety is important, but few people want a lecture about it. After all, safety isn't anything more than simple common sense, right? Well, maybe, but consider this: of the 300 children under the age of 5 who drown and the 2,300 other ones who end up in emergency rooms each year due to pool-related accidents, 77 percent are missing for 5 minutes or less before they are found in the pool. Less than 2 percent of those accidents involve children who are trespassing on the pool owner's property.

Based on statistics from the Consumer Product Safety Commission (CPSC), these facts and figures reveal two important points. One is that an accident can happen in less time than it takes for you to read this sentence. The other is that, more often than not, it isn't a child who is trespassing who gets into trouble. It is the pool owner's kids, grandkids, nieces, nephews, and friends' kids who get themselves into situations where they need an adult's help. So, yes, much of pool safety is common sense, but there is more to it than that. This chapter will present some ways for you to make your pool and spa safe for everyone. First, it will discuss how you can protect small children. Then it will address safety issues for anyone who uses the pool. For advice on what you should be aware of when using spas in particular, see page 215.

SAFETY AND CHILDREN

Children are cute, lovable, entertaining, and many other great things. But because they also tend to be inquisitive, fearless, unsteady on their feet, and fast, they need to be supervised constantly while in the pool or spa area. Adult supervision is your main defense against an accident. In addition, you can make the pool environment as safe as possible for them.

All Eyes

The best way to prevent small children from drowning or becoming injured in a pool is possibly the easiest—watch them at all times. As any parent or anyone who has ever taken care of young children can tell you, kids move a lot faster than you may think possible for their size. Unfortunately, they seem to get that speed at the expense of any sense of caution. If you need to go into the house—even for just a second—take the children with you. It's also a good idea to take a cordless or cell phone with you when you are outdoors and the kids are in the pool.

If you are having a large party, plan supervision as you would any other detail. There are many things that can distract you when you are entertaining. Keep nonswimming activities away from the pool to prevent accidents. You may even want to consider hiring a professional lifeguard.

Instruct Baby-Sitters. You are not the only one who has to be serious about safety. It is also imperative that those who take your place are just as cautious. Baby-sitters, whether they are teenagers from the neighborhood, older siblings, or even other adults, should receive a course in pool and spa safety from you. Set rules.

Nearby phone access, left, is always a good idea.

The edge of the pool, opposite, is clear and uncluttered by furniture to eliminate tripping hazards.

Fence Specifications

The opening between the bottom of the fence and the ground should be 4 inches or less. This small of a space will prevent a child from wiggling under and gaining entry to the pool or spa area.

Fences should be at least 48 inches high. They should be constructed so that handholds and footholds for climbing the fence and gaining entry into the pool area are eliminated. The distance between vertical fence members or

A barrier fence, right, can be softened in appearance by planting flowers and shrubs alongside it.

A mesh fence, below, closes off the pool area but not the attractive view into the yard.

Even an aboveground pool may have a fence. This fence is mounted to the top of the pool.

openings in the fence should not exceed 1¾ inches. This distance is based on the foot width of a young child and is intended to reduce the potential for a child to gain a foothold.

If the style of a fence places the tops of its horizontal members less than 45 inches apart, these members can be on the pool or spa side of the fence. If the distance between the horizontals is more than 45 inches, they can be placed on the side of the fence facing away from the pool. In this case, vertical members can be spaced up to 4 inches apart. This distance will keep children from passing between the vertical parts of the fence.

Chain-Link Fences. The mesh opening on chain-link fence should not exceed 1¼ x 1¼ inches. You can achieve this by installing a fence with openings that are that close together, or you can install vertical slats through the mesh to reduce the size of the openings. Secure the slats to the top and bottom of the fence, placing them so that the mesh openings are no larger than 1¾ inches.

Gates

As with the case of fences, gates should restrict children from entering the pool or spa area on their own. The gate should be self-closing and have a self-latching mechanism.

The ideal gate closes toward the pool, so if a child pushes against a gate that is unlatched, he or she will actually lock the gate. Place the latch at least 54 inches above the ground. If that is not possible, install the latch 3 inches down from the top on the pool side of the gate. This will prevent a small child from reaching up and unlatching the gate.

Fencing for Aboveground Pools

Because most aboveground pools are 48 inches high, they serve as their own barrier. Many pool manufacturers also sell fencing that mounts on the top of the pool wall. Deck kits that surround an aboveground unit usually include fencing. If the one you purchase does not, install a fence that is high enough to meet local codes—usually 36 inches. That means the final barrier will be 48 inches high (the height of the wall) plus 36 inches of fencing on top. This allows you to partially sink the pool into a sloped site. Keep less than 4 inches between the pool wall and the bottom of the fence.

Ladder and Stairs. Although the high walls of a typical aboveground pool present an adequate barrier to a small child, the pool's ladder or stairs present a weak link in the pool's overall security. Either surround the bottom of the stairs with a fence built to the specifications described, including a self-locking gate, or remove the stairs when the pool is not in use.

SAFETY FOR EVERYONE

A pool or spa in the yard will be the focal point of entertaining. As the owner you will be liable for the safety of your guests, so like it or not, it makes sense to lay down a few rules to keep everyone safe. It is also important to plan ahead when you have guests.

People will be barefoot while around the pool or spa, so use unbreakable dishes, cups, and utensils. It is also a good idea to keep the food and particularly the food-preparation areas away from the water.

Do not allow running around the pool, roughhousing, diving into shallow water or from the side of the pool, or any game that involves diving through an inner tube or some other toy. Diving games often lead to injury.

Drinking and drugs do not mix with swimming or soaking in a hot tub. Dealing with someone who has had too much to drink can be a sensitive situation. But the fact is, as the owner, you are responsible. If you would not let them drive home, don't let them in the water.

Rainstorms with lightning present dangerous situations. Get everyone out of the pool when lightning is in the area. Follow the procedure of some public pools, and clear the pool at the first sound of thunder or if you know a storm is about to hit. Keep everyone out of the water until the danger passes.

Pool Equipment and Accessories

All pool equipment and accessories perform specific functions. They will operate safely as long as you have installed and maintained them properly. See Chapters 3 (pages 60–81), 4 (pages 82–93), and 7 (pages 136–155) for details on proper installation and maintenance procedures. Here are a few basic safety concerns to increase your enjoyment of your pool or spa.

Filters, Pumps, and Heaters. Install or make sure your contractor installs equipment in accordance with manu-

A diving area requires deep water. Diving off the side of the pool should not be permitted.

POST RULES

AS THE OWNER, you are responsible for the safety of everyone who uses your pool. Post a set of rules for everyone to read and follow. Some examples include:

- No running around the pool
- No diving from the side of the pool or into shallow areas
- No unsupervised children in the pool
- No drinking and swimming
- No glass containers around the pool

facturer's instructions, including installation on a proper base, securing the equipment to the base, and proper electrical grounding. Follow specified maintenance procedures for equipment.

Grates and Drains. Keep the pool's inlet and outlet fittings, grates, skimmer, and main drain in place at all times. Drains should be equipped with a Safety Vacuum Release System. These devices automatically shut down the system should a swimmer become stuck to a drain due to suction. Swimmers with long hair should avoid all pool outlets.

Ladders, Steps, and Handrails. These items must be mounted securely. Regularly inspect them for sharp edges, loose nuts and bolts, and broken treads. Keep ladders and handrails unobstructed for safe use.

Diving Boards. Install them only on in-ground pools deep enough for diving. Industry standards call for diving equipment matched to the dimensions of the pool. Always consult a professional when selecting and installing diving equipment. Diving surfaces must have a slip-resistant covering. Keep the surfaces clean and in good repair. Never install diving equipment on an aboveground pool.

Sliding Equipment. As with diving equipment, sliding equipment must be matched to the pool. Check with a professional for information on the best slide for your pool and its optimal location. Follow the manufacturer's directions regarding installation, clearance over the water, and depth of the water around the slide. Keep the slide and ladder in good repair, checking regularly for missing treads, sharp edges, and loose nuts and bolts.

Diving and Sliding with Caution

Dive only into the deep end of pools designed for diving. Divers should know proper diving techniques: hold your head up; keep your arms extended in front of you; and steer up with your hands. Never dive into the shallow end of the pool. That sounds like common sense that everyone should know, but each year dozens of people suffer everything from cuts and bruises to serious head or neck injuries because they don't follow common sense.

Keep slides fun and safe. Anyone using a slide should either be sitting up or lying flat, belly down and head first. If you're using the latter position, keep your hands out in front and slide only into deep water. Unsupervised children should not use slides. A slide should not empty into the shallowest end of the pool, but if the water is very deep, permit only good swimmers to use it.

Do not allow anyone to use the slide as a diving platform, a temptation when the slide is high. Even when a slide is bolted to the deck, it is not intended for nor is it safe for diving from it. If you really want a slide, be cautious. Consider a model that has large rocks or some other landscaping element surrounding it. This may discourage inappropriate access or reckless behavior. Again, set strict rules about sliding, and enforce them.

A safe diving board shows no sign of warping or cracking and is firmly anchored into the pool deck.

DIVING DOS AND DON'TS

THE ASSOCIATION OF POOL AND SPA PROFESSIONALS offers the following dos and don'ts of diving:

- Do know the shape and depth of the pool before diving.
- Do plan the dive to avoid submerged obstacles, surface objects, and other swimmers.
- Do hold your head and arms up, and steer up with your hands.
- Do practice carefully before you dive.
- Do test the diving board for its spring before diving.
- Do dive straight ahead, not off to the side of the diving board.
- Don't drink and dive.
- Don't dive into an above-ground pool.
- Don't dive into shallow water.
- Don't dive across narrow parts of the pool.
- Don't engage in horseplay on diving boards.
- Don't do back dives.
- Don't try fancy dives.
- Don't dive headfirst through objects like inner tubes.
- Don't dive alone.

If it wears out, replace the nonskid material on top of the board. Buy a kit, which comes with manufacturer's directions.

SPA SAFETY

THE RULES that apply to pools, regarding adult supervision, fences, gates, proper installation and use of accessories and equipment, and safe use and storage of chemicals, apply to spas as well. But there are additional safety concerns for spa users to consider.

- Never let anyone, especially children, use the spa alone.
- Pregnant woman and people with heart disease, diabetes, or high or low blood pressure should not use a spa without consulting with their doctors.
- Keep a maximum water temperature of 104 degrees Fahrenheit.
- Keep a thermometer in the spa to monitor the temperature of the water.
- Limit soaking time to about 15 minutes. If you want to soak longer, leave after 15 minutes, cool down, and then return. Another option is to lower spa water temperature to about 98 degrees Fahrenheit.
- Don't use a spa if you have an open wound or sore.
- Never drink alcohol and use the spa. Alcohol increases body temperature and expands blood vessels. This, in combination with high water temperatures, can lead to dizziness, lightheadedness, or unconsciousness.
- If possible, have spa users shower with soap and water before entering the spa.
- Nonsanitary water can lead to skin rashes. Avoid cloudy or foaming water.
- Don't soak in a spa immediately after eating a heavy meal.

An indoor swim spa, above right, should be off limits to very young children. Keep the door locked.

A sturdy handrail, right, is a safety feature that makes it easier to enter or exit the hot tub.

CHAPTER 10

Soothing Saunas

A session in a sauna can relax you, invigorate you, and contribute to your overall well-being all at once. Most people have heard of saunas, but few in North America have experienced a true sauna or understand the concept.

A sauna is both an activity and a place. It is a ritualized dry-heat bath as well as the bathhouse itself. The sauna experience consists of sitting or lying in a heated environment where temperatures reach as high as 195 degrees Fahrenheit. Occasionally, a bather will ladle water onto hot stones to produce a sudden burst of steam. It is the steam that often causes people to confuse saunas with steam baths. But despite the periodic clouds of steam, the overall humidity in a sauna remains low—about 25-percent relative humidity as compared with 100-percent humidity in a steam bath. A true sauna session also includes a cooling down period, then a rest, followed by a repeat of the sauna/cool down cycle. (See "The Sauna Experience," on page 223.)

Finland is the birthplace of saunas. In that country, saunas are not considered luxuries the way that we think of a spa or whirlpool tub. They have been part of Finnish everyday life for over 2,000 years. The Finns use saunas for quiet contemplation, family and social gatherings, and even for business meetings.

The first saunas were probably caves that were heated by a wood fire. This produced both hot cave walls and a lot of smoke. Once the smoke cleared, people enjoyed the warmth radiating from the rock walls. Some sauna fanatics say the only true sauna is a smoke sauna *savusauna*. But that is a matter for debate. Even in Finland, where there are more saunas than cars, most saunas are smokeless and heated with electric heaters.

People enjoy saunas because they are relaxing and healthy. The heat rests tired muscles and may reduce inflammation. The experience can also relieve stress and tension. While taking part in the sauna ritual, the metabolic rate will increase, and your heart will get a light workout. In addition, your skin will perspire, removing dirt and grime from the pores. The result is clean skin with a healthy glow. Some people even believe that regular use of a sauna can help you to lose weight. Although a sauna session will sweat off some pounds, any weight loss is really water loss, and it won't last.

Spending a few minutes in a sauna adds a relaxing, healthy touch to your bathroom routine.

WHO SHOULD NOT USE A SAUNA

BECAUSE A SAUNA increases circulation and heart rates, pregnant woman and anyone with heart problems should consult a doctor beforehand. Children should never use a sauna unless an adult is present.

Do not use a sauna after drinking alcohol or after a heavy meal. The combination of heat and alcohol could make you fall asleep. Also, the increase in heat can interfere with normal digestion.

SAUNA ROOMS

The typical sauna is a small, insulated wood-lined room that contains benches, a waterproof floor, a heater, and a door that opens out so as not to use up valuable floor space inside the sauna. A door that swings out is also a safety precaution because it allows someone outside to help someone who passes out and falls against the door.

Saunas are made of wood, and many North American species are perfect for their construction. These include redwood, Western red cedar, and Alaskan yellow cedar. These softwoods have an attractive grain pattern, absorb humidity, and remain cool to the touch despite the intense heat of the sauna. Hardwoods tend to hold the heat and become uncomfortable to the touch after a short time.

The woods used in saunas are left unfinished. The high temperatures found in a sauna would harm wood sealers and varnishes.

Construction

You can build your own sauna, but a number of manufacturers sell complete units that you can assemble in your home. Prices vary from company to company, but for a small one-person sauna, expect to pay about $2,000 for a kit that includes a heater. Larger units that can accommodate seven or eight people can cost as much as $8,000 or $9,000. Although saunas are available in a variety of sizes, most units are 7 feet high, allowing them to fit in any interior space. A one-person sauna measures 3 x 4 feet, while a four-person model measures about 5 x 7 feet, with two levels of benches.

10

Soothing Saunas

A softwood sauna room includes benches that stay cool against your skin while you enjoy the therapeutic effects of the heater.

Precut Kits. A sauna kit is usually shipped in individual pieces and includes precut tongue-and-groove lumber for the walls and ceiling, lumber for the benches, and a door. Basic kits will have doors with plain glazing, but manufacturers also offer decorative etched-glass panels. In some cases, the kit also contains a heater, a light, and other accessories.

Kits usually contain materials for the interior of the sauna only. You must insulate, frame, and build the exterior of the unit, and provide a waterproof floor. Most manufacturers call for a concrete floor and provide some sort of covering for the floor, such as floorboards installed with spaces between them. A floor drain is helpful but not absolutely necessary for a residential sauna. However, your local building code may require a floor drain.

Prefabricated Saunas. These are complete units—interior and exterior—shipped in sections. You supply only the waterproof floor. Some manufacturers offer roof kits with their prefabricated saunas, making exterior installations possible. As with sauna kits, heaters are often part of the package but sometimes must be purchased separately. In either case, the wiring for the heater and lights is already installed in the walls, and all you need to do is hook up the appliances and fixtures.

Heaters

Sauna heaters consist of a heating element and a bin to hold a pile of rocks. True sauna rocks are igneous stones from Finland. The heater transfers its heat to the rocks, which in turn radiate their warmth into the room. The heaters are sized to match the room in which they will be

A prefabricated sauna is easy to install and can be located almost anywhere in the house.

This sauna design, left, leaves plenty of room for seating and has a centrally installed heater.

A stainless-steel heating unit, below left, is best placed on the floor in a corner of the sauna.

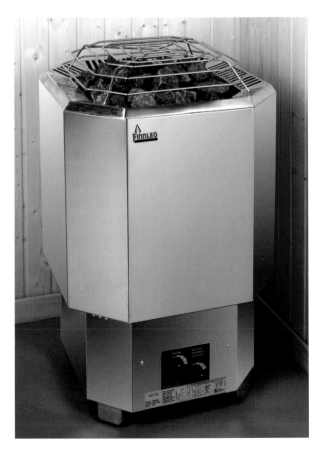

used. Most manufacturers provide sizing charts that show how much space their products can handle.

While you can buy wood-burning sauna heaters, most heaters run on electricity. The electric heating elements offer the advantage of being in direct contact with the rocks. The smallest heaters can operate on standard 120-volt circuits, but any sauna with over 100 cubic feet of space, which is any room built for more than one person, requires 240-volt service.

Smaller heaters can be mounted on a wall; larger units stand on the floor. A typical wall-mounted heater might measure 16 inches wide x 11 inches deep x 24 inches high. Floor models are usually deeper and up to 32 inches high. Most heaters come with a 60-minute timer.

Heaters typically require a preheat cycle of about 30 minutes. However, instant-heat units are now becoming available. There is no need to preheat them, so you can enjoy a sauna as soon as you get the urge.

Instant-heat units are insulated, fully enclosed units that are always on. You will incur the cost of providing electricity to the heater when it is not in use, but manufacturers say this cost is minimal. When you want to use the heater, you simply open the top of the unit and pour water onto the hot stones.

PLANNING YOUR SAUNA

As a rule of thumb, plan on providing 2 feet of bench space for each adult. Figure on 6 feet for someone who wants to lie down in the sauna. Most saunas consist of two levels of benches. Sauna users climb onto the lower level to reach the top level of the sauna. As mentioned above, the heat in the room will rise, so the hottest temperatures are usually found near the sauna ceiling.

For the complete sauna experience, consider the sauna room as part of a larger relaxation area. Other items to consider include a shower, dressing room, and cool-down room. If you place the sauna near a deck or patio, the outside area could serve as a cool-down or rest area.

Accessories

As with pools and spas, there are a variety of accessories available to enhance the experience. For practical purposes, you can replace the standard controls on the heater with digital controls that preset sauna temperatures and operate the lights as well. Some units constantly monitor temperature and humidity levels.

You can also buy decorative wall-hung thermometers. For the ritual of dousing the hot stones with water, sauna manufacturers offer a variety of decorative buckets and ladles. Most are made of wood, the traditional material used for these items, but you can buy copper buckets as well.

Also available are aromatic oils, soaps, and lotions. Many of these are birch scented to simulate the *vihtas*, or bundle of birch branches used in the traditional Finnish sauna.

Sauna accessories, such as brushes, hand massagers, and plush towels add to the overall experience.

Smart Tip

The ideal sauna height is about 7 feet. People sitting on the upper bench will enjoy maximum heat of about 165 to 195 degrees Fahrenheit with a minimum amount of preheat time. Eight-foot sauna ceilings increase heating time and waste energy.—D.S.

THE SAUNA EXPERIENCE

WHILE YOU ARE FREE to use the sauna any way that you wish, you will get the full benefit if you think about sauna sessions as a ritual that is set apart from the rest of your day.

Here is a possible routine based on the way saunas are used in Finland. Traditionally, people used twigs to stimulate circulation and exfoliate the skin. However, you can use a loofa or sponge.

• **HEAT UP.** Switch on the sauna heater; leave the room; and close the door. Most saunas take about 30 minutes to come up to desired temperatures. Many people say a temperature between 155 and 195 degrees Fahrenheit is ideal. Try different temperatures until you find what works for you. While waiting, many people like to take a quick shower.

Enter the sauna, and take your place on the benches. Sauna sessions can be solitary ventures or social occasions. In any case, the temperature is highest near the ceiling, so you should instruct children and the elderly to sit on the lower benches.

When you first enter the sauna, the humidity will be at about 5 to 10 percent. As you begin to perspire, the humidity in the room will rise. After a few minutes, ladle some water over the hot rocks to produce a burst of steam. If you are new to saunas, limit your session to about 10 minutes and work you way up to about 20 minutes.

• **COOL DOWN.** Leave the sauna, but keep the heater on. Bring your body temperature down by taking a shower, going for a swim, or if you are hearty enough, rolling around in the snow. The object is to cool down.

• **REST.** Now take a few minutes to relax. Lie down in a spot where you won't be disturbed. Plan on resting for as long as you were in the sauna.

• **DO IT AGAIN.** Repeat the process up to three times. The sauna will open your pores, releasing oils and dirt. After your final cool down, sponge off the grime and exfoliate with a loofa. Rest after your final cleansing. In Finland, people follow their sauna session with a light snack.

A large, lighted sauna can be used as a social place to share with friends.

resource guide

The following list of manufacturers and associations is meant to be a general guide to additional industry and product-related sources. It is not intended as a listing of products and manufacturers represented by the photographs in this book.

ASSOCIATIONS

AquaTech is a society that comprises over 120 pool builders. Its Web site shows a variety pool designs, ideas, and accessories, and will direct you to a builder in your area.
www.aquatechpools.com

Association of Pool and Spa Professionals (APSP), an international trade association, promotes the safety and proper maintenance of pools and spas. APSP also offers free consumer information on building and maintaining pools and spas.
2111 Eisenhower Ave.
Alexandria, VA 22314
Phone: 703-838-0083
www.nspi.org

California Redwood Association is a nonprofit trade organization that offers extensive technical information about redwood. The Association also has design and how-to help for a variety of outdoor structures.
Phone: 888-225-7339
www.calredwood.org

The Chlorine Institute, Inc., a membership trade association, focuses on the safe production, distribution, and use of chemicals, such as chlorine and sodium.
1300 Wilson Blvd.
Arlington, VA 22209
Phone: 703-741-5760
www.CL2.com

National Swimming Pool Foundation (NSPF), a membership organization, is committed to the enhancement of water safety. Its Web site includes a newsletter and membership information.
4775 Granby Cir.
Colorado Springs, CO 80906
Phone: 719-540-9119
www.nspf.com

National Swim School Association is a trade organization. Its Web site can direct you to qualified swim schools in your area.
www.nationalswimschools.com

BUILDERS AND SUPPLIERS

Anthony & Sylvan provides new pool and spa installations, modernizations of existing pools, equipment, service, supplies, and other backyard extras. Its Web site will direct you to a sales and design center in your area.
Phone: 877-891-7946
www.anthonysylvan.com

Aqua Swim'N'Spa, a division of Rio Plastics, sells a variety of therapeutic swim and spa combinations in different sizes.
P.O. Box 3707
Brownsville, TX 78523
Phone: 956-831-2715
www.rioswimspas.com

Bradford Products manufactures stainless-steel spas. The company also makes swim spas in a variety of styles.
710 Sunnyvale Dr.
Wilmington, NC 28412
Phone: 800-438-1669
www.bradfordproducts.com

Cascade Pools manufactures residential in-ground pools in a wide variety of styles.
6775 SW McEwan Rd.
P.O. Box 2049
Lake Oswego, OR 97035
Phone: 503-620-6174
www.cascadepoolsandspas.com

Comfort Line manufactures portable spas, saunas, and accessories for indoor or outdoor use.
Phone: 888-997-6366
www.comfortlineproducts.com

Custom Pools designs and builds pools and spas. The company's Web site offers information on residential swimming pools.
2225 Lafayette Rd.
Portsmouth, NH 03801
www.custompools.com

Dimension One Spas manufactures therapeutic spas in a variety of styles and sizes.
2611 Business Park Dr.
Vista, CA 92081
Phone: 800-345-7727
www.d1spas.com

Endless Pools, Inc., manufactures lap pools and hydrotherapy pools with an adjustable current for individual preferences.
200 E. Dutton Mill Rd.
Aston, PA 19014
Phone: 800-732-8660
www.endlesspools.com

Fox Pool Corp. constructs a broad line of in-ground vinyl pools and spas. They also sell a special line of pools that accommodate Amish living standards.
3490 Board Rd.
York, PA 17402
Phone: 800-723-1011
www.foxpool.com

Hot Spring sells portable spas, saunas, and pools.
1366 W. Valley Pwy.
Escondido, CA 92029
Phone: 877-821-5536
www.spasandtubs.com

Jacuzzi Whirlpool Bath manufactures luxury bathing equipment including outdoor spas, soaking and jetted bathtubs, and accessories.
Phone: 866-234-7727
www.jacuzzi.com

Kayak Pools builds aboveground pools. The company's Web site contains a catalog.
2000 Commerce Pkwy.
Lancaster, NY 14086
Phone: 800-639-5292
www.kayakpools.com

Lombardo Swimming Pool Co. builds in-ground pools that are designed to fit the landscape.
1501 Industrial Dr.
Matthews, NC 28105
Phone: 704-847-4648
www.lombardopools.com

Master Spas manufactures polymer indoor and outdoor spas in a variety of colors.
6927 Lincoln Pkwy.
Fort Wayne, IN 46804
Phone: 260-436-9100
www.masterspas.com

Medallion Pools offers a selection of in-ground pools, aboveground pools, spas, swim spas, and accessories.
840A West Roslyn Rd.
Colonial Heights, VA 23834
Phone: 800-367-3865
www.medallionpools.com

Mid-State Swimming Pools sells in-ground pools that are manufactured by various companies. They also offer products and replacement parts.
1303-B W. College St.
Murfreesboro, TN 37129
Phone: 615-890-0980
www.mid-statepools.com

Pacific Pools manufactures pools with a lifetime warranty. The Web site has a dealer directory.
8533 Transit Rd.
East Amherst, NY 14051
Phone: 716-636-1480
www.pacificpools.com

Paddock Pools specializes in the design and construction of commercial pools.
15120-C Southlawn Ln.
Rockville, MD 20850
Phone: 301-424-0790
www.paddockpools.com

Roberts Hot Tubs manufactures traditional barrel-style hot tubs in redwood, teak, and cedar. Its Web site includes a photo catalog of hot tub styles.
Phone: 800-735-5290
www.rhtubs.com

Sharkline, an aboveground swimming pool company, manufactures pools, liners, decking systems, and accessories. Its Web site offers technical and safety information to consumers.
Wilbar International, Customer Service
50 Cabot Ct.
Hauppauge, NY 11788
Phone: 631-951-9800
www.sharkline.co

Splash Superpools manufactures and sells portable, aboveground pools that are supported by steel for extra durability.
3912 E. Progress
N. Little Rock, AR 72114
Phone: 501-945-4999
www.splashpools.com

Thermospas custom designs and installs spas, hot tubs, and accessories.
Phone: 800-876-0158
www.thermospas.com

Tiger River Spas, a manufacturer of portable spas, offers a variety of styles and sizes. Its Web site shows the different models that are available to consumers.
Phone: 800-999-4688
http://tigerriver.hotspring.com

FURNITURE AND ACCESSORIES

Arch Wood Protection, Inc. manufactures pressure-treated wood for decks, landscaping, walkways, gazebos, fences, and picnic tables. Information and building plans are available through its Web site.
1955 Lake Park Dr., Ste. 100
Smyrna, GA 30080
Phone: 770-801-6600
www.wolmanizedwood.com

Aerotube Technology, LLC, manufactures pool shades and enclosures that block UV rays and screen out bugs. The company's Web site shows the possible applications of this accessory.
Phone: 877-477-4787
www.aerotube.com

AGI Group, Inc., offers a varied selection of patio umbrellas and retractable awnings.
Sarasota International Trade Center
1550 Global Ct.
Sarasota, FL 34240
Phone: 800-823-6677
www.shuttertime.com

Beckett Corporation sells water-gardening pumps, supplies, and accessories. A visit to the Web site may help you design and install your own pond.
5931 Campus Circle Dr. W.
Irving, TX 75063
Phone: 888-232-5388
www.beckettpumps.com

Cover Pools, Inc., a pool-cover company, specializes in the "Safe-T Cover", which is a winter, solar, and safety cover all in one.
66 E. 3335 South
Salt Lake City, UT 84115
Phone: 800-447-2838
www.coverpools.com

Elyria Fence, Inc., makes custom wood, aluminum, iron, chain-link, and polyvinyl fences in a variety of designs.
230 Oberlin-Elyria Rd.
Elyria, OH 44035
Phone: 800-779-7581
www.elyriafence.com

Frontgate sells and manufacturers products such as pool and spa accessories, outdoor furniture, and electronics.
5566 W. Chester Rd.
W. Chester, OH 45069
Phone: 888-263-9850
www.frontgate.com

Intermatic, Inc., manufactures a variety of control systems and timers for pools and spas, as well as a line of low-voltage lighting products.
Intermatic Plaza
Spring Grove, IL 60081
Phone: 815-675-7000
www.intermatic.com

Kingsley-Bate, Ltd., a teak furniture manufacturer, sells outdoor furnishings, including lounge chairs, dining sets, and benches.
7200 Gateway Ct.
Manassas, VA 20109
Phone: 703-361-7000
www.kingsleybate.com

Keystone Retaining Wall Systems, a division of Contech Construction Products, manufactures retaining walls for structural and landscape use.
4444 W. 78th St.
Minneapolis, MN 55435
Phone: 800-897-1040
www.keystonewalls.com

SPACAP.com offers spa covers that are specially designed for insulation.
Another Company
932 Birch Bay Lynden Rd.
Lynden, WA 98264
Phone: 877-772-2279
www.spacap.com

SR Smith manufactures pool accessories such as slides, diving boards, ladders, and rails for residential and commercial pools.
Phone: 800-824-4387
www.srsmith.com

Swim Ways Corporation manufactures numerous products for pool and water recreation, including swimmies, pool toys, lounges, games, learn-to-swim tools, and pool decor. Its products are sold in most pool supply and other stores.
5816 Ward Ct.
Virginia Beach, VA 23455
Phone: 800-889-7946
www.swimways.com

Telescope Casual Furniture, Inc., makes a wide array of patio, deck, and poolside furniture including chairs, tables, and umbrellas.
82 Church St.
Granville, NY 12832
Phone: 518-642-1100
www.telescopecasual.com

Recreation Supply Co. sells pool and spa water testing products, automatic pool cleaners, leaf skimmers and rakes, vacuum heads, hoses, and accessories.
P.O. Box 2757
Bismark, ND 58502
Phone: 701-222-486
www.recsupply.com

POOL AND SPA EQUIPMENT

Carefree Clear Water sells mineral ionization systems for pools and spas.
P. O. Box 304
Cornelia, GA 30531
Phone: 800-364-5710
www.carefreeclearwater.com

Hayward sells a variety of pool purification and circulation equipment including filters, valves, heaters, pumps, cleaners, and Goldline salt chlorinators.
www.haywardnet.com

Pentair Pool Products manufactures pool pumps, heaters, filters, and salt chlorinators. It also offers spa products and pool lighting systems.
1620 Hawkins Ave.
Sanford, NC 27330
Phone: 800-831-7133
www.pentairpool.com

Zodiac Pools, Inc., offers a variety of automatic pool cleaners, chlorinators, and purifiers. The company also manufacturers a line of aboveground pools available in a variety of sizes and shapes.
www.zodiacpools.com

MAINTENANCE PRODUCTS

AquaChek manufactures pool and spa test strips and kits, including salt-testing and water-balancing kits.
P. O. Box 4659
Elkhart, IN 46514-0659
Phone: 574-262-2060
www.aquachek.com

AstralPool, an international company, manufactures and markets water-treatment and pool products.
www.astralpool.com

Finlandia Sauna Products, Inc., manufactures Finnish softwood saunas, sauna heaters, and accessories.
14010-B S.W. 72nd Ave.
Portland, OR 97224-0088
Phone: 800-354-3342
www.finlandiasauna.com

Scandia Health Systems manufactures European-style saunas, steam baths, wooden tubs, and steam showers.
P.O. Box 636
Eagle, Idaho 83716
Phone: 877-467-2862
www.scandiahealth.com

Sussman Lifestyle Group manufactures and sells saunas and heaters.
Phone: 800-727-8326
www.sussmanlifestylegroup.com

SAUNAS

Baltic Leisure manufactures steam showers, pre-cut sauna kits, and prefabricated saunas in a variety of sizes for the home.
601 Lincoln St.
P. O. Box 530
Oxford, PA 19363
Phone: 800-441-7147
www.balticleisure.com

Finnleo Sauna and Steam offers an extensive line of saunas and products, including steam baths, steam and sauna rooms, heaters, and accessories that are designed to enhance the sauna experience.
575 E. Cokato St.
Cokato, MN 55321
Phone: 800-346-6536
www.finnleo.com

glossary

Acid demand The amount of acid required by a body of water to raise the pH to neutral (7).

Algaecides Chemical substances that kill algae or inhibit their growth in water.

Alkalinity The characteristic of water that registers a pH above neutral (7).

Backwash The process of running water through a filter opposite the normal direction of flow in order to flush out contaminants.

Balance The term used in water chemistry to indicate that the water is neither scaling nor corrosive when all components are mixed together.

Bather load The number of people who use a pool or spa. The bather load affects the routine maintenance.

Biguanide (polyhexamethylene biguanide) A sanitizing agent. Also called PHMB.

Blower An electromechanical device that generates air pressure to provide spa jets and rings with bubbles.

Bond beam The top section of a gunite pool that is more substantial than the rest of the pool. The bond beam supports the coping around the pool.

Bromine A disinfectant and oxidizer of organic materials. Often used as a replacement for chlorine.

Cartridge filter A filtration system made of polyester or other mesh material that removes contaminants.

Channeling Creation of a tube or channel in a sand or DE filter through which water will flow unfiltered.

Check valve A valve that permits the flow of water or air in only one direction through a pipe.

Chelating agent Chemical compounds that prevent minerals in solution in a body of water from precipitating out of solution and depositing on surfaces.

Chloramine Compound of chlorine when combined with inorganic ammonia or nitrogen.

Chlorinator A device that is part of the circulation system that delivers chlorine to the pool or spa water.

Chlorine A substance used to sanitize water by oxidizing (killing) bacteria; generally available in liquid, solid (tablets or sticks), and granular form.

Chlorine demand The amount of chlorine required (demanded) by a body of water to raise the chlorine residual to a level that sanitizes the water.

Combined available chlorine (CAC) Chlorine compounds that have been combined with organic matter.

Chlorine residual The amount of chlorine remaining in a body of water after all organic material (including bacteria) has been oxidized. Expressed in parts per million. The total chlorine residual is the sum of all available chlorine plus any combined chlorine (chloramine).

Diatomaceous earth (DE) filter A filtration system that uses diatomaceous earth, a substance made of billions of silicified algae and plankton skeletons (diatoms).

Diverter Plastic or bronze adapter valve that fits into a skimmer port to facilitate connection of a vacuum hose. The diverter can divert all suction to the skimmer, closing off the main drain or vice versa.

Electronic timers Solid-circuit devices that control the circulation systems of pools and spas.

Erosion feeder A device that allows water to slowly dissolve a sanitizing tablet. Some feeders are connected directly to the circulation system; others simply float on the surface of the pool.

Etching Corrosion of a surface by water that is highly acidic or low in total alkalinity.

Fiber optics A method of lighting whereby a beam of light travels through thin plastic cable.

Filter A medium that removes contaminants from the water in the circulation system of a pool or spa.

Free available chlorine (FAC) Also called "available chlorine." Chlorine in its elemental form, not combined with other elements, available for sanitation of water.

Gallons per minute (gpm) A unit of measurement.

Gas heater A pool heater that is fueled by natural or propane gas.

Ground-fault circuit interrupter (GFCI) A safety device that cuts the flow of electric current when it senses a difference in flow between the line and ground current.

Gunite A mixture of water, sand, and cement that is applied with a sprayer to form a pool or spa shell.

Hardness Also called "calcium hardness." The amount of dissolved minerals (mostly calcium and magnesium) in a body of water. In unbalanced water, high levels cause scale and low levels cause corrosion.

Heat pump A device that heats pools using the heat energy in the air to raise the temperature of a refrigerant. The refrigerant circulates through a compressor and heat exchanger where the heat in the refrigerant transfers to the water in the circulation system.

Hot tub A circular soaking tub made of wood. Hot tubs may or may not contain jets.

Hydrostatic valve A valve located under the main drain that relieves the buildup of ground water under the pool. Also known as a pressure-release valve.

Impeller A circular disk with raised vanes inside the pump that spins to create centrifugal force.

Inlet The entry point where water from the circulation system flows into the pool or spa.

Intermittent ignition device (IID) The electronic control and switch used in electronic ignition heaters to operate the control circuit and automatic gas valve.

Lap pool A long, narrow pool for swimming laps.

Multiport valve A valve having at least four positions.

Muriatic acid A chemical that lowers pH.

Neutral The pH reading at which a substance is neither acidic nor alkaline. Neutral pH is 7.

O-ring Rubber gasket used to create a waterproof seal in plumbing joints or between two parts of a device, such as between the lid and strainer pot on a pump.

Parts per million (ppm) A measurement of the concentration of a substance in a liquid.

PHMB See *Biguanide*.

pH Scale A scale that measures the relative acidity or alkalinity of soil or water. The pH scale is 0-14 where 7 is neutral, 0 is extremely acidic, and 14 is extremely alkaline.

Pressure gauge A device that measures air or water pressure. The pressure gauge on a filter can alert you to the need for filter maintenance.

Prime The process of initiating water flow in a pump to commence circulation by displacing air in the suction side of the circulation system.

Reagent A liquid or dry chemical formulated for water testing. A substance that reacts to another known substance, producing a predictable color in the water.

Sand filter A filtration system that uses pool-grade sand to remove contaminants from pool water.

Sanitizer Any chemical compound that oxidizes organic material to provide a clean water environment.

Sauna A chamber heated to a high temperature where intermittent steam is produced by pouring water over hot stones.

Scale Calcium carbonate deposits on pool surfaces.

Shocking See *Superchlorination*.

Skimmer A part of the circulation system that removes debris from the surface of the water.

Soda ash (sodium carbonate) A white powdery substance used to raise the pH of water.

Solar heater A system that collects energy from the sun and transfers heat to pool water. The solar collector panels are part of the pool's circulation system.

Spa A vessel designed for soaking. Spas contain jets that provide a variety of different massaging sensations.

Strainer basket A container found in skimmers and pool pumps that catches debris.

Superchlorination Periodic application of extremely high levels of chlorine (in excess of 3 ppm) to completely oxidize any organic material in a body of water and leave a substantial chlorine residual. Also called "shocking."

Swim spa A vessel larger than a soaking spa but smaller than a swimming pool that generates a strong current. People swim against the current as a form of exercise.

Total alkalinity (TA) The measurement of all alkaline substances in water.

Total dissolved solids A term describing all of the contaminants dissolved in water. At a certain point the amount of dissolved material affects water color.

Volute The chamber inside the pump that houses the impeller.

Weir The barrier in a skimmer over which water flows. A floating weir raises and lowers its level to match the water level in a pool or spa.

index

Metric Conversion

Length

1 inch	25.4 mm
1 foot	0.3048 m
1 yard	0.9144 m
1 mile	1.61 km

Area

1 square inch	645 mm^2
1 square foot	0.0929 m^2
1 square yard	0.8361 m^2
1 acre	4046.86 m^2
1 square mile	2.59 km^2

Volume

1 cubic inch	16.3870 cm^3
1 cubic foot	0.03 m^3
1 cubic yard	0.77 m^3

Common Lumber Equivalents

Sizes: Metric cross sections are so close to their U.S. sizes, as noted below, that for most purposes they may be considered equivalents.

Dimensional lumber	1 x 2	19 x 38 mm
	1 x 4	19 x 89 mm
	2 x 2	38 x 38 mm
	2 x 4	38 x 89 mm
	2 x 6	38 x 140 mm
	2 x 8	38 x 184 mm
	2 x 10	38 x 235 mm
	2 x 12	38 x 286 mm
Sheet sizes	4 x 8 ft.	1200 x 2400 mm
	4 x 10 ft.	1200 x 3000 mm
Sheet thicknesses	¼ in.	6 mm
	⅜ in.	9 mm
	½ in.	12 mm
	¾ in.	19 mm
Stud/joist spacing	16 in. o.c.	400 mm o.c.
	24 in. o.c.	600 mm o.c.

Capacity

1 fluid ounce	29.57 mL
1 pint	473.18 mL
1 quart	1.14 L
1 gallon	3.79 L

Weight

1 ounce	28.35g
1 pound	0.45kg

Temperature

Fahrenheit = Celsius x 1.8 + 32
Celsius = Fahrenheit - 32 x ⁵⁄₉

Nail Size and Length

Penny Size	Nail Length
2d	1"
3d	1¼"
4d	1½"
5d	1¾"
6d	2"
7d	2¼"
8d	2½"
9d	2¾"
10d	3"
12d	3¼"
16d	3½"

photo credits

Page 1–11: *all* LOOK Photography **page 13:** Brian Vanden Brink **page 14:** Brian Vanden Brink, builder: Axel Berg **page 15:** *top* Brian Vanden Brink; *bottom* courtesy of Endless Pools **page 16:** *top* Brad Simmons, landscape design: D&S Designs, builder: Real Log Homes; *bottom* Jerry Demoney/Stock Pile, Inc. **page 17:** Tria Giovan **page 18:** Mark Samu **page 19:** *top* John Parsekian; *bottom* Richard Felber **page 20:** Horticultural Photography **page 22:** Ken Druse **page 28:** Brian Vanden Brink, architect: Perry Dean Rogers and Partners **page 29:** Brian Vanden Brink **page 30:** Deborah Sherman **page 31:** *top* Brian Vanden Brink, architect: John Martin; *bottom* Deborah Sherman **page 32:** Brian Vanden Brink, architect: Sam Van Dam **page 33:** *top* courtesy of National Pool & Spa Institute; *bottom* Mark Samu **page 34:** Jerry Harpur, design: Prattial Gutierrez **page 35:** Richard Felber **page 37:** John Parsekian **page 39:** Brian Vanden Brink **page 40:** Beth Singer **page 41:** Mark Samu **page 42:** Randall Perry, builder: Witt Construction **pages 43–44:** *both* courtesy of National Pool & Spa Institute **page 44:** *top* Steven Wooster/Garden Picture Library, design: Anthony Paul; *bottom* Tim Griffith/Garden Picture Library **page 46:** Brian Vanden Brink, architect: Roc Caivano **page 47:** *top* carolynbates.com; *bottom* Brad Simmons, landscape design: Barry Wehrman, architect: Greg Staley **page 48:** Mark Lohman **page 49:** Anne Gummerson, architect: Wayne Good **page 50:** Ken Druse, design: William Wallis, ASLA **page 51:** *top* courtesy of Bradford Spas; *bottom* Jerry Harpur, design: Wayne Connor **page 52:** courtesy of Vaughan Pools **page 53:** Brett Drury **page 54:** *top* Tre Dunham; *bottom* Mark Lohman **page 55:** *top* Beth Singer; *bottom* Tria Giovan **page 56:** *top* Mark Samu; *bottom* Olson Photographic, LLC **page 57:** **top** Mark Samu, architect: Keller Sandgren; **bottom** Olson Photographic, LLC **page 58:** *top* Olson Photographic, LLC; *bottom* Todd Caverly, design: William Thompson Architects **page 59:** *top* Deborah Sherman; *bottom* Mark Samu **pages 60–61:** Brian Vanden Brink **page 63:** *top* Richard Felber; *bottom* Gary Bumgarner/Positive Images **page 64:** Bill Rothschild **page 67:** Brian Vanden Brink **page 70:** Bill Rothschild **page 71:** *all* courtesy of Hayward **page 75:** Mark Samu **page 76:** Karen Bussolini/Positive Images, landscape architect: Tramontano & Rowe **page 77:** courtesy of Cover Pools, Inc. **page 78:** Jerry Pavia **page 81:** Steven Wooster/Garden Picture Library, design: Di Farth Design **page 83:** Beth Singer **pages 84–85:** *left both* courtesy of Frontgate; *top* Phillip Ennis, design: Four Seasons Greenhouses; *right bottom both* courtesy of Master Spas **page 86:** *top* courtesy of Master Spas; *bottom* Jerry Harpur **page 87:** courtesy of Frontgate, manufacturer: Wild Ride Slides/Inter-Fab **page 88:** *both* carolynbates.com **page 89:** Brian Carter/Garden Picture Library **page 90:** *left & top right* courtesy of Zodiac, Inc.; *center right & bottom right* courtesy of

Frontgate **page 91:** *both* courtesy of Frontgate **pages 92–93:** *left* Mark Lohman; *center* Steven Wooster/Garden Picture Library, design: Michelle Osbourne; *top right* courtesy of National Pool & Spa Institute **page 95:** Todd Caverly, courtesy of Sunset Hill House **page 96:** *top* Deborah Sherman; *bottom* Lee Anne White/Positive Images **page 97:** davidduncanlivingston.com **page 98:** *bottom left* Jerry Pavia; *top right* Randall Perry, builder: Witt Construction **page 100:** davidduncanlivingston.com **page 101:** Thomas McConnell **page 102:** Olson Photographic, LLC **page 103:** Mark Lohman **page 104:** Tre Dunham **page 105:** Olson Photographic, LLC **pages 106–107:** *top* Chris Cooper; *bottom* John Parsekian/CH **page 108:** Lee Lockwood/Positive Images **page 109:** Steven Wooster/Garden Picture Library **page 111:** Richard Felber **page 113:** Brian Vanden Brink **page 114:** *both* Palma Allen **page 115:** Richard Felber **page 117:** Brigitte Thomas/Garden Picture Library **pages 118–119:** *all left* Mary Messenger; *right* Brett Drury **page 120:** Jerry Pavia **page 121:** Brian Vanden Brink **pages 122–123:** Steven Wooster/Garden Picture Library, design: Sir Mylles and John & Pauline Trengrove **pages 124–125:** davidduncanlivingston.com **page 126:** *top* courtesy of Fox Pools; *bottom* John Parsekian **page 128:** Jerry Harpur, design: Garret Eckbo for Sam Hellinger **pages 129–130:** *all* Palma Allen **page 132:** Jerry Pavia **page 133:** Brian Vanden Brink **page 134:** John Parsekian **page 135:** Ken Druse **pages 136–137:** Mark Samu, courtesy of Hearst Specials **page 138:** *left* Ken Druse; *right* John Parsekian/CH **page 139:** Jerry Harpur **page 140:** *all* John Parsekian/CH **page 141:** *top* John Parsekian/CH; *bottom* Richard Felber **page 142:** Richard Felber **page 143:** *all* John Parsekian/CH **page 144:** Ken Druse **page 145:** Brian Vanden Brink **pages 147–148:** *all* John Parsekian/CH **page 151:** John Ferro Sims/Garden Picture Library **page 152:** Phillip Ennis, architect: Steven Ackerman **page 153:** Mark Lohman **page 155:** Randall Perry **page 157:** Brian Vanden Brink **page 158:** *top* Tony Giammarino/Giammarino & Dworkin, design: Tom Speeches; *bottom* Jerry Harpur, design: Thomas Church **page 160:** Jerry Pavia **page 161:** *top* Jerry Harpur, design: Nadine Butler; *bottom* Mary Messenger **page 162:** Brian Vanden Brink, builder: Ron Forest Fences **page 163:** Todd Caverly, architect: William Thompson **page 164:** Phillip Ennis, architect: Brian Schuchardt **page 165:** courtesy of Hickson Corporation **page 166:** Michael Thompson **page 167:** Derek Fell **page 168:** Catriona Tudor Erler **page 169:** *left* Jerry Pavia; *right bottom to top* Catriona Tudor Erler; Jerry Pavia; Charles Mann; Jerry Pavia **pages 170:** *left both* John Parsekian/CH; *right all* Catriona Tudor Erler **page 171:** *all photos* Catriona Tudor Erler; *illustrations* Nancy Hull **page 172:** *all* courtesy of Intermatic **page 173:** *all* Brian C. Nieves/CH **page 174:** Richard Felber **page 175:** courtesy of Keystone

Retaining Walls **page 178:** Tony Giammarino/Giammarino & Dworkin **page 179:** *top* Ken Druse; *bottom* Richard Felber **page 180:** *top right* Richard Felber; *bottom right* Brad Simmons; *bottom left* Jerry Harpur, design: Villa Bebek **page 182:** Ken Druse **page 183:** *top* Richard Felber; *center* Jerry Harpur, design: Mary Effron; *bottom* Brian Vanden Brink **page 184:** *top* John Parsekian; *center* Tony Giammarino/Giammarino & Dworkin, design: Tom Speeches; *bottom* Jerry Harpur, design: Edna Walling **page 185:** Richard Felber **page 186:** *all* Catriona Tudor Erler **page 187:** Eric Crichton/Garden Picture Library **page 188:** *top* John Glover; *bottom* Jerry Harpur, design: Jeff Mendoza **page 189:** *all* Catriona Tudor Erler **page 190:** *left* Roger Foley; *right* Derek Fell **page 191:** Ken Druse **page 192:** Ken Druse **page 193:** *top* Harry Heit/Steve Katona's North Hill Water Gardens; *bottom* judywhite/Gardenphotos.com **page 194:** *top* David McDonald/Photo Garden Inc.; *bottom* Jerry Pavia **page 195:** J. Paul Moore **pages 196–197:** *top right & top left* Tria Giovan; *bottom right* Tony Giammarino/Giammarino & Dworkin; *bottom left* Mark Samu **page 198:** *top* Tony Giammarino/Giammarino & Dworkin; *bottom* Mark Samu **page 199:** *top* Mark Lohman; *bottom* Jerry Pavia **page 200:** *top* Jessie Walker; *bottom* Beth Singer **page 201:** *top* Tria Giovan, *bottom* Peter Leyden **page 203:** Todd Caverly, courtesy of Sunset Hill House **page 204:** Phillip Ennis, design: Audio Command Systems **page 205:** Bill Rothschild, builder: The Horowitz Organization **pages 206–207:** *top right* courtesy of Frontgate, manufacturer: Panasonic; *bottom right* Brad Simmons, builder: Wilderness Log Homes; *top left* Tony Giammarino/Giammarino & Dworkin, design: Tom Speeches **page 208:** courtesy of Cover Pools **page 209:** *both* Tria Giovan **page 210:** *top* Horticultural Photography; *bottom* davidduncanlivingston.com **page 211:** courtesy of Sharkline Pools **page 212:** Tony Giammarino/Giammarino & Dworkin, design: Tom Speeches **page 213:** courtesy of SR Smith **page 214:** carolynbates.com **page 215:** *top* carolynbates.com; *bottom* courtesy of Thermospas **page 217:** carolynbates.com **page 218:** Robert Perron **page 219:** Jessie Walker **page 220:** courtesy of Baltic Leisure **page 221:** *both* courtesy of Finnleo **page 222:** Phillip Ennis, design: Greenbaum Interiors/Lynn Cone **page 223:** courtesy of Finnleo **page 224:** courtesy of National Pool & Spa Institute **page 225:** *top* courtesy of Bradford Spas; *bottom* courtesy of Keystone Retaining Walls **page 226:** courtesy of Endless Pools **page 227:** *top* courtesy of Sharkline Pools; *bottom* courtesy of Thermospas **page 228:** *top* courtesy of Cover Pools, Inc.; *bottom* courtesy of Frontgate, manufacturer: Wild Ride Slides/Inter-Fab **page 229:** courtesy of SR Smith **page 230:** courtesy of National Pool & Spa Institute **page 231:** *top* courtesy of Finnleo; *bottom* courtesy of Cover Pools

Have a home gardening, decorating, or improvement project? Look for these and other fine **Creative Homeowner books** wherever books are sold.

An impressive guide to more than 100 flowering plants. More than 500 color photos. 208 pp.; 9" × 10"
BOOK #: 274032

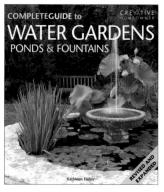

A comprehensive tool for the aspiring water gardener. Over 600 color photos. 240 pp.; 9" × 10"
BOOK #: 274458

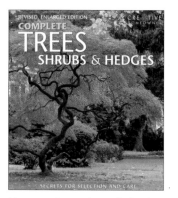

How to select and care for landscaping plants. Over 700 color photos and illustrations. 240 pp.; 9" × 10"
BOOK #: 274222

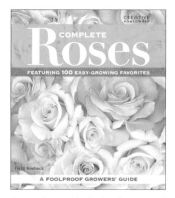

A growing guide for beginners and experienced gardeners. Over 280 color photos. 176 pp.; 9" × 10"
BOOK #: 274061

Guide to creating beautiful gardens. Over 1,000 photos and illustrations. 400 pp.; 9" × 10"
BOOK #: 274021

Inspiring ideas to achieve stunning effects with the landscape. Over 350 photos. 208pp.; 8½" × 10⅞"
BOOK #: 274154

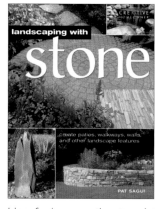

Ideas for incorporating stone into the landscape. Over 400 color photos and illos. 224 pp.; 8½" × 10⅞"
BOOK #: 274172

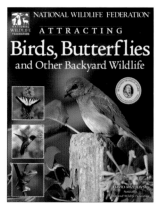

Wildlife-friendly gardening practices and projects. Over 200 color photos and illos. 128 pp.; 8½" × 10⅞"
BOOK #: 274655

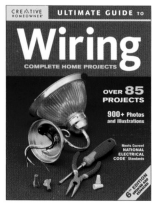

New, updated edition of best-selling house wiring manual. Over 850 color photos. 320 pp.; 8½" × 10⅞"
BOOK #: 278242

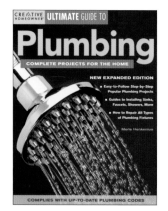

Take the guesswork out of plumbing repair. More than 800 photos and illustrations. 288 pp.; 8½" × 10⅞"
BOOK #: 278200

How to work with space, color, pattern, and texture. Over 500 photos. 304 pp.; 9¼" × 10⅞"
BOOK #: 279679

All you need to know about designing a bath. Over 260 color photos. 224 pp.; 9¼" × 10⅞"
BOOK #: 279239

For more information, and to place an order, go to **www.creativehomeowner.com**